►Select Readings

Pre-Intermediate

Linda Lee
Erik Gundersen

OXFORD
UNIVERSITY PRESS

OXFORD
UNIVERSITY PRESS

198 Madison Avenue, New York, NY 10016 USA
Great Clarendon Street, Oxford OX2 6DP England

Oxford New York
Auckland Bangkok Buenos Aires Cape Town
Chennai Dar es Salaam Delhi Hong Kong
Istanbul Karachi Kolkata Kuala Lumpur
Madrid Melbourne Mexico City Mumbai
Nairobi Sao Paulo Shanghai Singapore
Taipei Tokyo Toronto

and an associated company in Berlin

OXFORD is a trademark of Oxford University Press.

ISBN 0–19–437700–8

Copyright © 2002 Oxford University Press

**Library of Congress Cataloging-in-Publication
Data**

Lee, Linda, 1950–
    Select Readings—Pre-Intermediate / by Linda Lee
and Erik Gundersen.
        p./cm.
    ISBN 0–19–437700–8
    1. English language-Textbooks for foreign
speakers.
    2. Readers. I. Gundersen, Erik. II. Title.

PE1128.L426 2002
428.6'4-dc21   00–029125

No unauthorized photocopying

Select Readings—Pre-Intermediate
Editorial Development, Project Management,
and Production: Marblehead House, Inc.
Assistant Editor: Phebe Szatmari
Designer: Susan Brorein
Production Manager: Shanta Persaud
Production Coordinator: Eve Wong
Composition & Prepress Services: Compset, Inc.
Cover design: Tom Hawley, Hawley Design
Cover photo: Yu Jun-Chin/Top Photo Corp./Henry
Westheim Photography

Printing (last digit): 10 9 8 7 6 5 4 3 2 1

Printed in China.

ACKNOWLEDGEMENTS

***The publishers would like to thank the
following for their permission to reproduce text
excerpts:***

"Mika's Homestay in London," "Cell Phones: Hang Up
or Keep Talking," and "How Safe Is Nuclear Power?"
adapted with permission from *Mini-World
Magazine.*
"How to be a Successful Businessperson" adapted
with permission from *The Wall Street Journal.*
Eastern Edition [Staff produced copy only] by Jeffrey
A. Tannenbaum. Copyright 1996 by DOW JONES &
CO INC. Reproduced with permission of DOW
JONES & CO INC in the format Textbook via
Copyright Clearance Center.
"Tonic Water, Please" adapted from an article by
Tetsuya Saruhashi. Used with permission from the
author.
"The Ghost Pilot" reproduced with permission from
Dorling Kindersley, Ltd.
"Helping Others" adapted with permission from
Habitat for Humanity International, based on the
article "Helping Others Sends Concrete Message"
that appeared in the April/May 2000 issue of *Habitat
World.*
"Vanessa-Mae: A 21st Century Musican" adapted with
permission from Weigl Educational Publishers
Limited.
"A Day in the Life of a Freshman" adapted with
permission from the author.
"Great Places to Visit" adapted with permission from
National Geographic Taiwan.

Studio photography by: Rick Ashley
Location photography by: Rick Ashley and Adam
Brown

***The publisher would like to thank the following
for their permission to reproduce photographs:***

Prof. Joseph Jacobson: ©Webb Chapelle, 1995–1999;
Kazi Food portrait: Adam Brown/winstonwest.com;
Lockheed 1011 jet courtesy of Lockheed Martin
Aeronautics Company; nuclear power plant:
www.comstock.com; Taroko Gorge and
Highway©Ron Watts/CORBIS; Trail in Bamboo
Forest©Ron Watts/CORBIS; General Electric
Console Television©Schenectady Museum, Hall of
Electrical History Foundation/CORBIS; National
Palace Museum in Taipei©Kevin R. Morris/CORBIS;
Vanessa-Mae Holding Her Violin©S.I.N. /CORBIS;
Vendor Sells to Baseball Fans©Kelly-Mooney
Photography/CORBIS; Pedestrians Crowding a
Street©Macduff Everton/CORBIS; Baseball Fans in
Fukuoka Stadium©Michael S. Yamashita/CORBIS;
Diners Eat at Night Market in Taiwan;©Michael S.
Yamashita/CORBIS; photo of Mariko Asano courtesy
of Habitat World Magazine; Beach at Lan Yu©Yu Jun-
Chin/Top Photo Corp./Henry Westheim Photography;
Reactor Core and Cooling Pool©Yann Arthus-
Bertrand/CORBIS; Yami hair dance©Cheng Chi
Hai/Top Photo Corp./Henry Westheim Photography.

Many thanks to Zubair Kazi and Chris Scanlan of
Kazi Foods for their help with the photo of Mr. Kazi
in Chapter 4 and to George Cary and the staff of
Finz Restaurant in Salem, Massachusetts for their
cooperation in setting up the photograph for
Chapter 5.

Dictionary definitions adapted from the Oxford
American Wordpower Dictionary.

► Acknowledgments

The publisher would like to thank the following teachers whose comments, reviews and assistance were instrumental in the development of *Select Readings*:

Ann Mei-Yu Chang	Greg Stinnett	Patricia Pei-Chun Che
Ann-Marie Hadzima	Hideaki Narita	Paul Cameron
Beatrice Hsiao-Tsui Yang	Hsiu-Chieh Chen	Pei-Yin Lu
Brett Reynolds	Hyun-Woo Lee	Peng-Hsiang Chen
Chia-Yi Sun	Jessica Hsin-Hwa Chen	Richard Solomons
Chi-Fan Lin	Jong-Bok Kim	Robin Cheng-Hsing Tsai
Ching-Kang Liu	Jong-Yurl Yoon	Russell Lefko
Christine Chen-Ju Chen	Joyce Yu-Hua Lee	Sherry Hsin-Ying Li
Christopher E. Cuadro	Kabyong Park	Stella Wen-Hui Li
Chuan-Ta Chao	Kozuko Unosawa	Stephen Mendenhall
Colin Gullbery	Kun-liang Chuang	Stephen Slater
David W.Y. Dai	Maggie Sokolik	Steven Donald
Douglas I-Ping Ho	Makoto Shimizu	Susan Shu-Hua Chou
Ellen Margaret Head	Maureen Chiu-Yu Tseng	Tsuh-Lai Huang
Florence Yi-Hui Chiou	Meredith Pike-Baky	Won Park
Frances J. Shiobara	Moasung Lin	Ying-Chien Chang
Fujiko Sano	Monica Li-Feng Kuo	Yu-Chen Hsu

The authors would like to thank the following OUP staff for their support and assistance in the development of *Select Readings*:

Chris Balderston	JJ Lee	Paul Riley
Julia Chang	Chang Oh Lim	Sumio Takiguchi
Tina Chen	Hannah Lee	Alison Kane
Coco Cheng	Kevin Park	Aya Iwamura
Ted Yoshioka		

Special thanks to Marblehead House and Chris Foley for all of your insights, guidance, and suggestions for change throughout the editorial process. Working with you has been a great pleasure.

▶ Contents

▶ Scope and Sequence

	Content	Reading Skill	Building Vocabulary	Language Focus
Chapter 1 Are You Getting Enough Sleep?	The importance of sleep	Using context clues	Learning words in context	Understanding the present perfect and simple past
Chapter 2 Mika's Homestay in London	Studying in an English-speaking country	Understanding words with more than one meaning	Keeping a vocabulary log	Giving reasons with *because* and *since*
Chapter 3 The Book of the Future	Technology for future books	Previewing	Using compound nouns	Using comparative forms of adjectives
Chapter 4 How to Be a Successful Businessperson	Building a successful business	Making inferences	Making a word form chart	Using infinitives
Chapter 5 Tonic Water, Please	Communicating in a foreign language	Scanning	Understanding prefixes	Connecting ideas with *and, but*, and *however*
Chapter 6 Cell Phones: Hang Up or Keep Talking?	The dangers of cell phone use	Understanding the difference between facts and opinions	Expressing certainty and uncertainty	Understanding what pronouns refer to
Chapter 7 The Ghost Pilot	A ghost story	Summarizing	Learning synonyms	Using *must have* + past participle

▶Scope and Sequence

	Content	Reading Skill	Building Vocabulary	Language Focus
Chapter 8 Helping Others	Volunteering	Identifying the topic and main idea	Using prefixes: *un-, im-, in-, ir-*	Understanding gerunds
Chapter 9 Baseball Fans Around the World	The behavior of baseball fans	Making predictions	Grouping words and phrases	Using the verbs *see, hear, watch,* and *feel* + object + *-ing* form
Chapter 10 Vanessa-Mae: A 21st Century Musician	A young musician's life	Dealing with unfamiliar words	Understanding suffixes	Showing a contrast with *although*
Chapter 11 How Safe Is Nuclear Power?	Nuclear power	Writing margin notes	Learning word forms	Using a verb + *that* clause
Chapter 12 Love at First Sight	Falling in love	Asking yourself questions while you read	Using a learner's dictionary	Using the past continuous
Chapter 13 A Day in the Life of a Freshman	A university student's life	Using context clues	Understanding two-word verbs	Expressing cause and effect with *so* + noun/adjective + *that*
Chapter 14 Great Places to Visit	Travel destinations	Reading words in chunks	Using context to know if a word is a noun or a verb	Understanding *-ing* clauses

► Introduction

To the Teacher

Select Readings is a series of reading texts for pre-intermediate and intermediate students of English. In both books high-interest reading passages serve as springboards for reading skills development, vocabulary building, language analysis, and thought-provoking discussions and writing.

In **Select Readings—Pre-Intermediate**, the readings address a wide range of fresh and engaging topics, like how to be a successful businessperson, electronic books of the future, love at first sight, and baseball fans around the world.

Components

The complete **Select Readings—Pre-Intermediate** program includes the following components:

- *Student Book*

- *Quizzes and Answer Key.* This is available for downloading at *www.oup.com/elt/selectreadings*. This easy-to-use instructor's companion includes an answer key for all activities in the Student Book and a reproducible, one-page quiz for each chapter.

- *Cassette.* An accompanying audio cassette features recordings of all of the reading passages in the book.

General Approach to Reading Instruction

The following principles have guided our approach throughout the development of **Select Readings:**

- **Readers become engaged with a selection when they are asked to respond personally to its theme.** While comprehension questions help students see if they have understood the information in a reading, discussion questions ask students to consider the issues raised by the passage.

- **Readers sharpen their reading, vocabulary-building, and language analysis skills when tasks are tied directly to the content and language of each reading passage.** *Select Readings—Pre-Intermediate* introduces students to reading skills such as previewing and making inferences, to vocabulary-building strategies such as learning synonyms and keeping a vocabulary log, and to language study topics such as using infinitives and giving reasons with *because* and *since*.

- **Good readers make good writers.** Reading helps students develop writing skills, while writing experience helps students become better readers.

- **Background knowledge plays an important role in reading comprehension.** An important goal of *Select Readings* is to illustrate how thinking in advance about the topic of a reading prepares readers to better comprehend and interact with a text.

Chapter Overview

Each chapter in *Select Readings* includes the eight sections described below. Suggested time frames for covering the material are also given.

1. Opening Page (5 to 15 minutes)

The purpose of this page is to draw readers into the theme and content of the chapter.

Teaching Suggestions:

- Call students' attention to the *Chapter Focus* box. Give them a chance to think about the content and skills they are about to study and to set their own learning goals for the chapter.

- Ask students to identify what they see in the photo(s) or artwork on the page and guess what the chapter is about. Have them read the quotation, restate it in their own words, and then say if they agree with it. Finally, ask what connection there might be between the image(s) and the quotation.

2. Before You Read (30 to 40 minutes)

Questions in many of the *Before You Read* sections ask students to reflect on their prior knowledge of each chapter's topic. Giving students time to think about and discuss these questions is an essential part of helping them activate their background knowledge on each topic. In Chapter 4 and beyond, the majority of *Before You Read* sections include a *Previewing Chart*. To complete this chart, students are asked to scan the reading for important names, places, and words. Using the information they have found, students predict what the reading will be about. Effective readers use pre-reading skills like scanning to get an initial feel for the content and organization of the reading passage.

Teaching Suggestions:

- Make sure that students understand the purpose of the *Before You Read* activities. Explain that activating prior knowledge will help them to better comprehend the reading passage.

- Encourage student participation in the activities by having people work in small groups to complete the activities.

- React to the content of students' ideas rather than to the grammatical accuracy of their responses.

3. Reading Passage (45 to 60 minutes)

In general, the readings become increasingly longer and more complex as the chapters progress. To help students successfully approach each passage, we have provided the following support tools:

Vocabulary glosses. Challenging words and expressions are glossed throughout the readings. In many cases we have glossed expressions (e.g., *making a profit*) instead of individual vocabulary items (e.g., *profit*). This approach helps students develop a better sense of how important context is to understanding the meaning of new words.

Culture and Language Notes. On pages 151–163, students will find explanations for cultural references and language usage that appear in blue print in the readings. Notes are provided on a wide range of topics from cultural information on American high schools, to geographical references such as London, and to famous people such as Mozart.

Numbered lines. For easy reference, every fifth line of each reading passage is numbered.

Recorded reading passages. Students can listen to all of the reading passages on the audio program that accompanies *Select Readings—Pre-Intermediate.* Listening to someone reading a text aloud helps language learners see how words are clustered in meaningful groups, thus aiding comprehension.

Teaching Suggestions:

- Encourage students to read actively. Circling words, writing questions in the margins, and taking notes are three ways in which students can make reading a more active and meaningful experience.

- Make sure students know how to use the vocabulary glosses, *Culture and Language Notes*, and other support tools to assist them in the reading process.

- Encourage students to use context to guess the meaning of unfamiliar words.

- Play the recorded version of the reading passage and ask students to listen to how the reader groups words together. As they listen to the recording, students lightly underline or circle the groups of words.

4. After You Read: Understanding the Text (30 to 45 minutes)

Following each passage, there are two to four post-reading activities that give students the chance to clarify their understanding of the text and discuss the issues raised in the reading. The comprehension questions test students' understanding of the facts, basic concepts, and new vocabulary presented in the passages. Questions in the *Consider the Issues* section ask students to talk about ideas introduced in the reading.

Teaching Suggestions:

- Get students to discuss their reaction to the readings in pairs or groups. The process of discussing questions and answers gives students an opportunity to check their comprehension more critically and analyze their reactions to the passages.

- Show students the value of returning to the reading again and again to answer the comprehension and discussion questions. Ask them to point out the specific places in the reading where they have found answers to the questions posed.

- If time permits and you would like students to have additional writing practice, ask them to write an essay or a journal entry on one of the questions in the *Consider the Issues* section.

5. Reading Skill (20 to 30 minutes)

At the beginning of each *Reading Skill* section, students encounter a short explanation of the skill in focus and, when appropriate, an example of how that skill relates to the reading in the chapter. The task following this explanation asks students to return to the reading to think about and apply a new reading skill.

- Discuss the general purpose of developing reading skills. The more students understand the rationale behind acquiring these critical skills, the more motivated they will be to develop and refine them.

- Review the explanations and sample sentences at the beginning of each *Reading Skill* section before asking students to tackle the questions that follow. Encourage them to ask any questions they have about the explanations or examples.

- Reflect with students on the ways in which they can apply the reading skills they have learned in each chapter to other reading passages and to other reading genres.

6. Building Vocabulary (20 to 30 minutes)

Reading extensively is an excellent way for students to increase their vocabulary base. Considering this, we pay careful attention to developing students' vocabulary building skills in each chapter of **Select Readings.** Learning words in context, understanding prefixes, using a learner's dictionary, and a variety of other vocabulary-building skills are taught throughout the book. Like the reading skill activities, each *Building Vocabulary* section starts out with a short explanation and, when appropriate, examples of the skill in focus. In the activity that follows the explanation, students often scan the reading to gather and analyze various types of words. In Chapter 2 and beyond, the final task in each *Building Vocabulary* activity invites students to record six new words or phrases they have learned in the *Vocabulary Log* found on pages 169–175. This activity encourages students to record and remember the vocabulary items that are important to them personally.

Teaching Suggestions:

- View the explanations and sample sentences at the beginning of each *Building Vocabulary* section before asking students to tackle the questions that follow. Encourage them to ask any questions they have about the explanations or examples.

- Show students the value of returning to the reading to find an answer whenever they are unsure of a vocabulary-related question.

- Encourage students to write down new words and phrases that are important to them in the *Vocabulary Log* on pages 169–175.

- Discuss the value of using an English-English learner's dictionary to find the meanings of unfamiliar words.

7. Language Focus (20 to 30 minutes)

The final skill-building section in each chapter calls attention to important grammatical structures and functions that occur with some degree of frequency in the reading passage. The goal of this section is to focus students' attention on critical grammar points as they occur in context.

Teaching Suggestions:

- Review the explanations and sample sentences at the beginning of each *Language Focus* section before asking students to answer the questions that follow. Encourage students to ask any questions they have about the explanations or examples.

- Invite students to talk about what they already know about the language point in focus. Many students know a great deal about grammar and are pleased to demonstrate this knowledge.

- Underscore the fact that the *Language Focus* sections are intended to help students review language they have already learned in the context of a reading passage. It can be very valuable for students to see the ways in which the grammatical structures they have studied appear naturally in real-life selections.

8. Discussion and Writing (45 to 60 minutes)

At the end of each chapter, students have an opportunity to talk and write about a variety of issues. The questions in this section provide students with a chance to broaden their view on the topic of the reading and to address more global issues and concerns. Students can write on a sheet of paper or in a notebook.

Teaching Suggestions:

- When time permits, let students discuss a question a second time with a different partner or group. This allows them to apply what they learned in their first discussion of the question.

- Choose one or more of the questions in this section as an essay topic for students.

Each chapter ends with a chart of useful *Words to Remember*. This chart summarizes the key words and phrases students should be able to recognize after completing each chapter.

This project grew out of our deep and profound love for reading, and our desire to share this love of reading with our students. In developing **Select Readings,** we have enjoyed the process of talking to teachers all over the world about the types of reading selections they feel their students enjoy the most, and learn the most from. We hope that you and your students enjoy teaching and learning with **Select Readings—Pre-Intermediate.**

Linda Lee

Erik Gundersen

Chapter ▲ **1** # Are You Getting Enough Sleep?

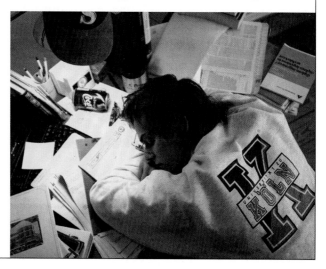

Chapter Focus

CONTENT:
The importance of sleep

READING SKILL:
Using context clues

BUILDING VOCABULARY:
Learning words in context

LANGUAGE FOCUS:
Understanding the present perfect and simple past

Before You Read

A. Check (√) your answers to these questions about sleep.

1. How many hours a night do you usually sleep?
   - ☐ fewer than 6 hours a night
   - ☐ between 6 and 8 hours a night
   - ☐ more than 8 hours a night

2. How do you feel when you wake up in the morning?
   - ☐ great   ☐ okay   ☐ terrible

3. How often do you feel sleepy during the day?
   - ☐ often   ☐ sometimes   ☐ almost never

B. Pair work. Compare answers. Do you have the same sleep habits?

A: I usually sleep fewer than 6 hours a night.
B: | Me too.
      | Really? I usually sleep more than 8 hours.

C. What do you think? Read these statements and guess True or False. Check (√) your guesses. Then read pages 3–4 and check your answers.

	True	False
1. Scientists don't know why we need to sleep.	☐	☐
2. It's possible to stay awake for one week.	☐	☐
3. It's unhealthy to go without sleep.	☐	☐

D. Group work. Compare your answers with your classmates. Then read pages 3–4 and check your answers.

ARE YOU GETTING ENOUGH SLEEP?

*Note: Explanations for words in **blue** type can be found in the Culture and Language Notes on pages 151–163.*

1   What happens if you don't get enough sleep? Randy Gardner, a **high school** student in the United States, wanted to find out. He designed an experiment[1] on the effects of sleeplessness[2] for a school science project. With doctors watching him carefully, Gardner stayed
5   awake for 264 hours and 12 minutes. That's eleven days and nights without sleep!

What effect did sleeplessness have on Gardner? After 24 hours without sleep, Gardner started having trouble reading and watching television. The words and pictures were too blurry.[3] By the third day,
10 he was having trouble doing things with his hands. By the fourth day, Gardner was hallucinating. For example, when he saw a **street sign,** he thought it was a person. He also imagined[4] he was a famous **football** player. Over the next few days, Gardner's speech[5] became so slurred that people couldn't understand him. He also had trouble
15 remembering things. By the eleventh day, Gardner couldn't pass a counting test.[6] In the middle of the test he simply stopped counting. He couldn't remember what he was doing.

When Gardner finally went to bed, he slept for 14 hours and 45 minutes. The second night he slept for twelve hours, the third night
20 he slept for ten and one-half hours, and by the fourth night, he had returned to his normal sleep schedule.

Even though Gardner recovered[7] quickly, scientists believe that going without sleep can be dangerous. They say that people should not repeat Randy's experiment. Tests on white rats have shown how
25 serious sleeplessness can be. After a few weeks without sleep, the

---

[1] **experiment**   a scientific test
[2] **effects of sleeplessness**   things that happen when you don't get enough sleep
[3] **blurry**   difficult to see
[4] **imagined**   thought
[5] **speech**   way of talking
[6] **a counting test**   saying numbers in order: 1, 2, 3, 4, etc.
[7] **recovered**   returned to normal

rats started losing their fur.[8] And even though the rats ate more food than usual, they lost weight. Eventually[9] the rats died.

30 During your lifetime, you will probably spend 25 years or more sleeping. But why? What is the purpose of sleep? Surprisingly, scientists don't know for sure.[10] Some scientists think we sleep in order to replenish[11] brain cells. Other scientists think that sleep helps the body to grow and to relieve stress.[12] Whatever the reason, we know that it is important to get enough sleep.

After You Read

Understanding the Text

A. True or False? Read the statements and check (√) True or False.

	True	False
1. Randy Gardner studied the effects of sleeping too much.	☐	☐
2. During the experiment, Gardner slept for several hours every night.	☐	☐
3. During the experiment, Gardner had trouble speaking clearly.	☐	☐
4. It took two weeks for Gardner to recover from the experiment.	☐	☐
5. Going without sleep is not dangerous for white rats.	☐	☐
6. Scientists are not sure why we need to sleep.	☐	☐
7. In the first paragraph, the words "find out" (line 2) mean *learn* or *discover.*	☐	☐
8. In the second paragraph (line 14) the word "slurred" means *easy to understand.*	☐	☐

Work with your classmates to correct the false statements.

---

[8] **fur**   hair on an animal's body

[9] **eventually**   after some time

[10] **for sure**   definitely

[11] **replenish**   build new; renew

[12] **relieve stress**   to remove or get rid of negative feelings

B. Consider the issues. *Work with a partner to answer the questions below.*

1. What are the effects of sleeplessness? List three more ideas from the reading passage.

POSSIBLE EFFECTS OF SLEEPLESSNESS
• You might have trouble seeing clearly.
• You might _____
• You might _____
• You could _____

2. **Pair work.** Think of three more possible effects of sleeplessness.

Example
A: You might have trouble driving a car.
B: That's right. And you could have trouble . . .

    a. You could _____

    b. You might _____

    c. _____

3. What is your opinion of Gardner's experiment? Check (✓) one or more statements or write your own.
    ☐ I think it was a dangerous experiment.
    ☐ I think it was an interesting experiment.
    ☐ I don't think the experiment was very scientific.
    ☐ I would like to know more about Gardner's experiment.
    ☐ _____

Share your opinion with your partner and tell why.

Example: *I think it was an interesting experiment because I learned a lot about the importance of sleep.*

Using context clues[13]

You don't need to understand the exact meaning of every new word. Instead, you can guess the general meaning of new words by looking at the context — the words before and after the new word, and in the sentences before and after the new word.

Example: *Gardner **stayed awake** for 264 hours. That's eleven days and nights <u>without sleep.</u>*

If you don't know the words "stayed awake," you can guess the meaning from the context clue "without sleep."

A. <u>Underline</u> the context clues that help you guess the meaning of the **boldfaced** words.

Example: *How did sleeplessness **affect** Gardner? After 24 hours without sleep, <u>he had trouble reading.</u>*

1. After 24 hours without sleep, Gardner had trouble reading and watching television. The words and pictures were too **blurry.**

2. By the fourth day, Gardner was **hallucinating.** For example, when he saw a street sign, he thought it was a person.

3. Over the next few days, Gardner's speech became so **slurred** that people couldn't understand him.

B. Use context clues to guess the general meaning of the **boldfaced** words. Circle your answer.

1. The price of clothing was so **reasonable** that we bought a lot of things. (cheap / expensive)

2. I felt so **at ease** on the airplane that I was able to go to sleep. (comfortable / uncomfortable)

3. The test was so **tough** that no one passed it. (easy / difficult)

4. We went to a **trattoria** after work. I ordered pasta, and he had a salad. (a place to work / a place to eat)

5. You will need a very sharp knife to **slice** those potatoes. (cut / wash)

---

[13] **clues**   things that help you find something or solve a problem

Building Vocabulary

Learning words in context

It's a good idea to learn a new word together with the words around it (the context). Below are some examples of the words that we often use with *sleep*.

go to sleep   get a good night's sleep
go without sleep   spend hours sleeping
get enough sleep   sleep schedule

A. Complete each question with a word from the box below. (More than one answer may be possible.)

enough	schedule	spend	to	without

1. What time do you usually *go* _____ *sleep*?

2. What time did you *go* _____ *sleep* last night?

3. Did you *get* _____ *sleep* last night?

4. How long can you *go* _____ *sleep*?

5. Do you usually *get* _____ *sleep* on weeknights?

6. Did you _____ *more than 50 hours sleeping* last week?

7. Do you have a regular or irregular *sleep* _____?

8. Do you have the same *sleep* _____ every day?

B. Pair work. Ask a partner the questions in Activity A.

A: What time do you usually go to sleep?
B: I usually go to sleep at 10:30.

Language Focus

Understanding the present perfect and simple past

At the beginning of a conversation, we often use the present perfect + *ever* to ask a general question about someone's past experiences. *Ever* means "at any time before now."

Examples: ***Have you ever slept*** *until noon?*
**   *Have you ever gone*** *to sleep in class?*

(See page 168 for a list of past participles for irregular verbs.)

To ask questions about a specific time or experience in the past, we use the simple past tense.

Example:
   A: *Have you ever gone for 24 hours without sleep?*
   B: *Yes, a few times.*
   A: *How did you feel?*
   B: *Terrible.*

A. Complete each pair of questions with a word in parentheses. Then ask a partner the questions.

   1. (sleep / slept / sleeping)

   a. Have you ever _____ for more than 12 hours?

   b. Why did you _____ for so long?

   2. (Have / Did / Has)

   a. _____ you ever slept for fewer than 6 hours?

   b. _____ you feel bad the next day?

   3. (gone / go / going)

   a. Have you ever _____ without sleep for more than 24 hours?

   b. Why did you _____ without sleep?

   4. (spend / spent / spending)

   a. Have you ever _____ 12 hours sleeping?

   b. Why did you _____ so much time sleeping?

B. Talk to different classmates. Find someone who answers "Yes" to each question below. Then ask the follow-up question.

   Example: A: *Have you ever slept on a waterbed?*[14]
      B: *Yes, I have.*
      A: *Was it comfortable?*
      B: *No. It was uncomfortable.*

---

[14] **waterbed**   a bed filled with water that moves when you lie on it

QUESTION	CLASSMATE'S NAME		FOLLOW-UP QUESTION	CLASSMATE'S ANSWER
Have you ever . . .				
slept on a waterbed?	_____	→	Was it comfortable?	_____
slept on an airplane?	_____	→	Were you comfortable?	_____
slept in a tent?	_____	→	Did you like it?	_____
fallen asleep during class?	_____	→	Did your teacher notice?	_____
had trouble going to sleep?	_____	→	What did you do?	_____

Discussion & Writing

A. Keep a sleep schedule for one week. Then answer the questions below.

	What time did you get up in the morning?	Did you feel sleepy during the day?	When did you go to bed at night?
Monday			
Tuesday			
Wednesday			
Thursday			
Friday			
Saturday			
Sunday			

1. Which night did you get the least sleep? Were you very sleepy the next day?

2. Which night did you sleep the most? How did you feel the next day?

3. Did you get enough sleep during the week? Why or why not?

B. Choose one of the questions below and answer it in writing.

1. What are the effects of going without drinking water?

2. What are the effects of going without food?

3. What are the effects of eating more than you need?

4. What are the effects of running 10 kilometers?

5. What are the effects of watching television all day?

Example:

What are the effects of going without drinking water?

After a few hours, you will begin to feel thirsty. Your mouth will feel dry too. After a few more hours, you might start to feel tired and dizzy. Soon you won't be able to do anything. If you go without water for too long, you will die.

WORDS TO REMEMBER		
NOUNS	VERBS	ADJECTIVES
experiment	find out	blurry
effects (of)	go without	dangerous
stress	have (trouble)	reasonable
	imagine	normal
	pass (a test)	
	recover (from)	
	spend (time)	

Chapter 2 ▲
Mika's Homestay in London

We travel to learn.

—Maria Mitchell,
U.S. astronomer
(1818–1889)

Chapter Focus

▼

CONTENT:
Studying in an English-speaking country

READING SKILL:
Understanding words with more than one meaning

BUILDING VOCABULARY:
Keeping a vocabulary log

LANGUAGE FOCUS:
Giving reasons with *because* and *since*

Before You Read

A. Imagine you are going to study in another country. Check (√) your answer to the question below and then tell your classmates.

Where would you like to live?

☐ in a hotel

☐ in a university dormitory

☐ with a host family (a family from that country)

☐ other: _____

> **Example:** *I would like to live with a host family.*

B. The author of the next reading lived with a host family in England. What would you like to know about her experience? Add two of your own questions to the list below.

QUESTIONS	ANSWERS
1. Did she enjoy staying with a host family?	
2. Did she live in London?	
3. Did she like the food in England?	
4.	
5.	

C. Read pages 13–14 and look for answers to the questions in Activity B. Write them in the chart above.

MIKA'S HOMESTAY[1] IN LONDON

by Mika Tanaka

*Mika Tanaka, a college student from **Japan**, had a wonderful homestay in **London**. She lived with a British family and studied English for a month.*

1   "What do you want for your 19th birthday?" my parents asked me. "A ring," I replied. However, instead of a ring, my parents gave me a one-month homestay in London.

    On February 11, I left Japan. On the plane, I worried about being all
5   alone[2] there — a stranger to London. But when I met the Flannery family (my host family), their warm welcome[3] made me feel at ease.[4] Both my host father and mother were very kind and treated me like their own daughter.[5]

Getting Ready to Go

    Before going to London, I did some research on English schools in
10   London and chose Oxford House College, mainly because it had reasonable fees. Also, there weren't many Japanese students at Oxford House.

    I took my parents' advice and requested that my homestay family have both a mother and a father, be native-born,[6] non-smoking,
15   middle-class British people, and live near a subway station. I later found that this was very good advice, since some of my friends at the English school were having problems with their host families.

Living in London

    Potatoes! It took me a little time to get used to[7] the many kinds of potato dishes served: fried potatoes, steamed potatoes, sliced
20   potatoes, and different-colored potatoes. My host mother was a good cook. She made delicious pasta and chicken dishes and even cooked rice for me.

---

[1] **homestay**   a period during which a visitor in a foreign country lives with a local family

[2] **all alone**   by myself; without someone I know

[3] **warm welcome**   friendly greeting

[4] **feel at ease**   feel comfortable

[5] **treated me like their own daughter**   were kind and good to me, like I was their own daughter

[6] **native-born British people**   people born in England

[7] **get used to**   become comfortable with

Nadiege, a French girl, was another homestay student living with us, and we went around London together. On Saturdays, my host
25 family would have a party at home with friends or family. When we returned from touring London, Nadiege and I would join the party. On Saturday evenings, Mr. and Mrs. Flannery would go to their favorite **pub**[8] to spend time together.

Although I selected a school with few Japanese students, there were
30 still at least two in each class. In class, I tried to speak a lot, but many Japanese students didn't use their English very much (even if they had large vocabularies), and spoke only Japanese with their friends.

Sometimes, I asked other people their impressions of[9] Japan. "Japanese people work too hard," said my French friend. My teacher
35 thought that Japanese people were very rich. I did not agree with these points,[10] but I was interested in knowing what foreign people thought. One month in London made me realize that speaking English was very important, because it is the language that people from many countries use the most. I would like to be more open-minded about
40 people from different countries, like my host family is.

After You Read

Understanding the Text

A. **Vocabulary check.** What is the correct meaning of the italicized words? Underline your answer.

1. The word *"replied"* in line 2 means (answered / asked / done).

2. The word *"reasonable"* in line 11 means (expensive / free / not expensive).

3. The word *"requested"* in line 13 means (asked / said / refused).

4. The word *"found"* in line 16 means (heard / read / realized).

5. The words *"went around"* in line 24 mean (avoided / toured / talked about).

---

[8] **pub**   a place where British people eat and drink
[9] **their impressions of**   their ideas about; what they think of
[10] **points**   ideas

B. True or False? Read the statements below and check (√) True or False.

	True	False
1. For her 19th birthday, Mika asked for a homestay in London.	☐	☐
2. She went to England with a friend.	☐	☐
3. Mika lived with a host family for two months.	☐	☐
4. She decided to study at Oxford House College because it wasn't expensive.	☐	☐
5. Mika did things in London with the Flannerys' youngest daughter.	☐	☐

Work with your classmates to correct the false statements.

C. Summarize. Read the summary, or main points, of Mika's story below and add the missing words.

> *Summary*
>
> For her 19th birthday, Mika Tanaka's parents sent her to
> L_____ . While she was there, she lived with a middle-
> class British f_____ . Her host f_____ and
> m_____ , Mr. and Mrs. Flannery, were very kind to Mika,
> and she felt relaxed with them. The Flannerys taught her a lot
> about British food and they invited her to a p_____ at
> their house every Saturday. Mika studied E_____ while
> she was in London and in class she tried to s_____ a lot.

D. Consider the issues. Work with a partner to answer the questions below.

1. Do you think Mika Tanaka would agree or disagree with the opinions below? Check (√) *Agree* or *Disagree* under "Mika."

Opinions	Mika Agree	Mika Disagree	Me Agree	Me Disagree
a. You should do some research before you travel abroad.	☐	☐	☐	☐
b. It's good to live with a host family.	☐	☐	☐	☐

Opinions	Mika		Me	
	Agree	*Disagree*	*Agree*	*Disagree*
c. Traveling abroad is a good way to learn English.	☐	☐	☐	☐

Do *you* agree with these opinions? Check (√) *Agree* or *Disagree* under "Me."

2. Mika made several important decisions before she went to London. For each decision, list an advantage and disadvantage.

Example: *Mika's decision: She decided to live with a host family that had both a mother and father.*

Advantage: She would experience living in a traditional British family.

Disadvantage: She would not experience a family setting different from her own in Japan.

a. Mika's decision: She decided to go to a school with few Japanese students.

Advantage: _____

Disadvantage: _____

b. Mika's decision: She decided to go to London alone.

Advantage: _____

Disadvantage: _____

Reading Skill

Understanding words that have more than one meaning

Many words in English have more than one meaning. You may know *one* meaning of a word, but it might not be the correct meaning for the word in that sentence. Use context clues to understand the correct meaning.

Example: I **run** about 10 kilometers a week.

A river **runs** past my house.

How many software programs is your computer **running?**

A. What does the word **like** mean in these questions? Match each word to dictionary definition 1, 2, or 3 below. Circle your answer.

1. Do you **like** potatoes?   1   2   3

2. Who do you look more **like** — your mother or father?   1   2   3

3. Do you feel **like** you need to sleep right now?   1   2   3

4. Would you like to try a dangerous sport **like** skydiving?   1   2   3

5. What does your best friend **like** to do?   1   2   3

6. Do you have an older sister who acts **like** she's your mother?   1   2   3

Dictionary definitions

- **like** *verb* [T] (not in the continuous tenses) **1** to find somebody or something pleasant; to be fond of somebody or something: *He's nice. I like him a lot.* The opposite is **dislike.** **2** to want: *How do you like your steak done, sir?*

> **Would like** is a more polite way to say "want": *Would you like to come to lunch on Sunday? I would like some more cake, please. I'd like to speak to the manager.*

- **like** *prep.* **1** similar to somebody or something: *He looks like his father. Their car is like ours. With a coat of paint it will look like new.* **2** showing what is usual or typical for somebody: *It was just like him to be late.* **3** in the same way or manner as somebody or something: *Stop behaving like kids. That's not right. Do it like this.* **4** for example: *They enjoy most team games, like football and baseball.*

- **like** *conj.* **1** in the same way or manner as: *She can't draw like her sister can.* **2** (informal) *as if: She acts like she's the boss. I felt like I was going to die.*

from the *Oxford American Wordpower Dictionary*

Pair work. Now ask a partner questions 1 to 6 above.

A: Do you like potatoes?
B: Yes, I like potatoes, especially french fries.

B. Mika Tanaka uses the word **like** three times (lines 7, 39, and 40.) What does it mean in each context? Share ideas with your classmates.

1. In line 7, *like* means _____

2. In line 39, *like* means _____

3. In line 40, *like* means _____

Building Vocabulary

Keeping a vocabulary log

It's a good idea to record important words in a vocabulary log like the one on pages 169–175. Here are some tips for recording new words.

1. Record a new word in context (with the words before or after it).

were very **kind**	**fried** potatoes
had **reasonable** fees	good **advice**

2. Use a new word to tell about something in **your** life.
   I don't like **fried** potatoes.
   My school has **reasonable** fees.

A. Rewrite these statements with information about yourself. Use the underlined words in your sentences.

1. Mika's host father and mother <u>were very **kind** to</u> her when she lived at their house.

   Example: *My grandparents were very kind to me when I was a child.*

   _____

   _____

2. The Flannerys <u>gave</u> Mika <u>a warm **welcome**</u> when she arrived in London.

   _____ gave me a warm welcome when

   _____

3. Mika wanted to study at a school that <u>had **reasonable** fees.</u>

   _____

   _____

B. Look back at the reading to find the missing word in each phrase below. Record the phrases in the vocabulary log on page 169. Then use the phrases in a sentence about yourself.

1. d_____ *some research* (line 9)

2. *middle-class* p_____ (line 15)

3. *treated me* l_____ (line 7)

4. *took my parents'* a_____ (line 13)

5. *hold a* p_____ (line 25)

6. *having problems* w_____ (line 17)

Language Focus

Giving reasons with <u>because</u> and <u>since</u>

We often use *because* or *since* when we want to give a reason for something.

Examples:

- Mika chose Oxford House College **because there weren't many Japanese students there.**

- Mika was happy she chose her host family carefully **since some of her friends were having problems with their families.**

A. Choose a reason. Complete each statement with a reason from the list on the right.

Sentence		Reasons
1. Mika went to London	_____	because she wanted to spend time with her husband.
2. Mika decided to study English at Oxford House	_____	because they lived with the same homestay family.
3. Mika got to know Nadiege	___1___	because it was her 19th birthday present.
4. Mika asked English people their impressions of Japan	_____	since they treated her like their daughter.
5. Mrs. Flannery went to a pub on Saturday evenings	_____	because she wanted to know what foreigners thought.
6. Mika felt comfortable with Mr. and Mrs. Flannery	_____	since it wasn't expensive.

B. What's your reason? Complete these sentences with information about yourself.

1. I want to travel to _____ because _____
   (place)

   _____

2. I think it's important to study _____ since _____.
   (school subject)

   _____

3. I got up at _____ o'clock this morning because _____.
   (number)

   _____

Discussion & Writing

A. What would your ideal host parents be like? Check (√) your answers below. Then, add two of your own ideas.

> ### MY IDEAL HOST PARENTS WOULD . . .
>
> ☐ *be native-born*
> ☐ *be non-smokers*
> ☐ *be middle-class*
> ☐ *be rich*
> ☐ *be good cooks*
> ☐ *be able to speak my language*
> ☐ *not be able to speak my language*
>
> ☐ *live near a subway station*
> ☐ *have lots of parties*
> ☐ *have children my age*
> ☐ *treat me like their son or daughter*
> ☐ _____
> ☐ _____

Write 4 to 5 sentences about your ideal host parents. Then read your sentences to a classmate.

Example:

My ideal host parents would be friendly. They would also live in a nice neighborhood and have lots of parties. They would . . .

B. Group work. What are some good reasons for studying abroad? Think of a way to complete each sentence below. Then compare your ideas with another group's.

Example: *It's a good idea to study abroad because you can learn to cook different kinds of food.*

It's a good idea to study abroad because . . .

- you can learn to _____.
- you can learn about _____.
- you can see _____.
- you can meet _____.
- you might become _____.

WORDS TO REMEMBER		
NOUNS	**VERBS**	**ADJECTIVES**
advice	do (research)	alone
impressions	get used to	delicious
	have (a party)	middle-class
	realize	reasonable
	reply	
	select	
	treat (someone) like	
	worry about	

Chapter ▲ 3 The Book of the Future

Prof. Joseph Jacobson
of the Massachusetts Institute of Technology

Necessity is the
mother of invention.

—*Thorstein Veblen,*
U.S. economist and
social philosopher
(1857–1929)

Chapter Focus

CONTENT:
Technology for future books

READING SKILL:
Previewing

BUILDING VOCABULARY:
Using compound nouns

LANGUAGE FOCUS:
Using comparative forms of adjectives

Before You Read

A. Pair work. What do you think? Read these questions and check (√)
Yes or No in Column 1 under "Our answers."

	Our answers		The writer's answers	
	Yes	*No*	*Yes*	*No*
1. Will people still read books in the year 2050?	☐	☐	☐	☐
2. Will books be made of paper in the future?	☐	☐	☐	☐
3. Will computers replace books in the future?	☐	☐	☐	☐

B. Compare answers with another pair.

> A: We think people will still read books in the year 2050.
> B: We do, too.
>   Really? We don't think they will.

C. Read the next article to find the writer's answers to the questions in
Activity A. Record the writer's answers in the second column of the
chart above.

Reading Passage

THE BOOK OF THE FUTURE

1   Will people still read books 100 years from now? A few years ago,
many people would have said *no*. It seemed likely[1] that computers and
the **Internet** would replace books. Now, however, most experts[2] think
that books are here to stay.

5   There are a number of reasons why computers won't replace
books entirely.[3] One reason is that books on paper are much cheaper
than computers. Books don't need a power source[4] either. You can

---

[1] **likely**   probable, almost certain

[2] **expert**   a person who knows a lot about something

[3] **entirely**   completely; altogether

[4] **a power source**   a battery or something else to provide energy

read a book for as long as you want and wherever you want. You never have to worry about losing power. Also, many people feel more comfortable reading words in a book than reading words on a computer screen. It's less tiring to the eyes.

Will books in the future be similar to the books you can buy today? The answer to that question is *no*. In the future, you may only need to buy one book. With this one book, you will be able to read novels,[5] plays, and even today's newspaper. It will look like today's book, but it will be electronic.[6]

One of the people working on the book of the future is Professor Joseph Jacobson from the **Massachusetts Institute of Technology** in the U.S. Professor Jacobson's book will have a small button on the side. When you press the button, words will instantly appear on the page. When you want to read a different story, you can push the button again and a new story will quickly appear.[7]

What is the technology behind[8] Professor Jacobson's book? Two important inventions[9] will make this new kind of book possible: electronic ink and radio paper. Electronic ink — or "e-ink" — is a liquid that can be printed on paper, metal, or anything else. E-ink looks and feels like printed words on paper. Unlike regular ink, however, words in e-ink are not permanent. They can be changed by pushing a button. When you push the button, all of the words on the page go away and new words appear.

The other new development[10] is radio paper. This paper looks and feels like a page in a book. In reality, however, radio paper is made of plastic.

Professor Jacobson calls his book of the future "the last book." This book, he says, will be the last book you will ever need.

---

[5] **novels**   fiction; books that tell stories that aren't true
[6] **electronic**   controlled by a computer
[7] **appear**   become visible; come into sight
[8] **behind**   making possible; supporting
[9] **inventions**   new things
[10] **new development**   new thing

After You Read

Understanding the Text

A. True or False? Read the statements and check (√) True or False.

	True	False
1. Electronic books will be like the books we have today.	☐	☐
2. You will be able to read many different stories in one electronic book.	☐	☐
3. You will be able to get the news in an electronic book.	☐	☐
4. The words in an electronic book will be permanent.	☐	☐
5. Radio paper is made of paper.	☐	☐

Work with a partner to correct the false statements.

B. Vocabulary check. Use context clues to choose the correct meaning of the italicized words. Circle the letter of the best answer.

1. The words *are here to stay* in line 4 mean . . .

    a. are nearby   **b.** are useless   **c.** won't disappear

2. The phrase *a number of* in line 5 is similar to the word . . .

    a. all   **b.** one   **c.** many

3. The word *press* in line 20 means . . .

    a. push   **b.** iron   **c.** pull

4. The word *instantly* in line 20 is similar to . . .

    a. very quickly   **b.** very slowly   **c.** seriously

5. The word *permanent* in line 28 means . . .

    a. powerful   **b.** serious   **c.** unchanging

C. Consider the issues. Work with a partner to answer the questions below.

1. What are the advantages and disadvantages of the e-book? Write these six ideas in the appropriate column of the chart below. Then add one more advantage and disadvantage.

- ~~An e-book will need a power source.~~
- It will be easy to use.
- Students won't need to carry a number of books to class.
- We won't need to cut down trees to make the paper.
- It could stop working.
- The words aren't permanent.

ADVANTAGES OF THE E-BOOK	DISADVANTAGES OF THE E-BOOK
_____	An e-book will need a power source.
_____	_____
_____	_____
_____	_____
_____	_____

2. Complete each sentence with a reason from the list on the right.

Sentences about e-books

Reasons

a. Electronic paper will be more expensive than regular paper because . . .

_____ it will look and feel like a regular book.

b. You will only need one book in the future because . . .

_____ you will own just one book.

c. E-ink is more useful than regular ink because . . .

__*a*__ it will be made of plastic.

d. People will feel comfortable reading an e-book because . . .

_____ it isn't permanent.

e. You won't need a bookshelf[11] in the future because . . .

_____ you will be able to change the stories in the book.

---

[11] **bookshelf**   a wood or metal structure where you put many books

Previewing

Pre means *before*. *View* means *to look at*. Before you read something, it's important to look it over, or preview it. When you preview a reading, you do three important things:

1) You identify the topic.
2) You think about what you already know about the topic.
3) You ask yourself questions about the topic.

Doing these three things will help you understand a reading better.

A. Follow these instructions to identify the topic of the paragraph below.

1. Look at the title of the paragraph below. (Don't read the paragraph.) Based on the title only, what do you think the paragraph is about?

E-Books

The book of the future will be made with <u>radio paper</u> and electronic <u>ink</u>. <u>Radio paper</u> has a coating of millions of tiny <u>capsules</u>. Inside each <u>capsule</u>, there is a dark liquid and hundreds of <u>white balls</u>. An electrical charge can make the <u>white balls</u> move to the top of the <u>capsule</u>. This makes the <u>"ink"</u> look white. An electrical charge can also make the <u>white balls</u> move to the bottom of the <u>capsule</u>. This makes the <u>"ink"</u> look black. When the <u>capsules</u> are charged in a pattern, they form letters on the page.

2. *Key words* are words that appear several times in a paragraph. In the paragraph above, the key words are underlined. Based on the key words <u>only</u>, what do you think the paragraph is about?

a. the history of radio paper and electronic ink

b. how radio paper and electronic ink work

c. how to use an e-book

Compare your answer with a partner.

B. Make a Know/Want to Know chart. Answer questions "a" and "b" below.

KNOW	WANT TO KNOW
a. What do you already know about the topic of the paragraph? Add two ideas.	b. What do you want to know about the topic of the paragraph? Add one question.
Electronic ink is a liquid. _____ _____	*What liquid is in electronic ink?* *What is in the capsules?* _____

C. Read the paragraph on page 27 and look for answers to the questions in the Know/Want to Know chart. Share your answers with a partner.

Building Vocabulary

Using compound nouns
We often use two nouns together. Sometimes the two nouns are written as one word.

Examples: *football, lifetime, textbook, homestay*

Sometimes the two nouns are written separately.

Examples: *high school, bank loan, convenience store*

A. Match the nouns that go together. Write the words. (More than one answer may be possible.)

1. computer • • station _____

2. news • • cells _____

3. brain • • screen _____

4. radio • • paper _____

5. power •   • sign   _____

6. street •   • family   _____

7. host •   • game   _____

8. subway •   • source   _____

B. Complete these phrases with words from the reading selection on pages 23–24. Then record the phrases in your vocabulary log on page 170.

1. here to *s*_____ (line 4)

2. *n*_____ a power source (line 7)

3. press the *b*_____ (line 20)

4. the *t*_____ behind (line 23)

5. looks and feels *l*_____ (lines 31–32)

Language Focus

Using comparative forms of adjectives

We use the comparative form of an adjective when we compare two things.

Form: cheap ⟶ cheaper

            big ⟶ bigger

            pretty ⟶ prettier

            expensive ⟶ more expensive

            comfortable ⟶ more comfortable

Examples:

- Books are **cheaper** than computers.

- People feel **more comfortable** reading words on paper than reading words on a screen.

A. What is the comparative form of these adjectives in Chapters 1–3?

1. sleepy _____   **5.** kind _____

2. warm _____   **6.** famous _____

3. dangerous _____   **7.** serious _____

4. delicious _____   **8.** reasonable _____

B. How was the first television different from today's television? Study the photograph below. Use the comparative forms in the Word Box to write three sentences.

Word Box
bigger
smaller
better
heavier
more convenient
more difficult to watch

Example: *The screen of the first television was much smaller.*

1. _____

2. _____

3. _____

Discussion & Writing

A. Choose one item in the box or think of your own invention or place. List five ways you hope it will be different in the future.

cars	universities	telephones	libraries
airplanes	computers	televisions	movie theaters

Examples: *I hope cars will be safer in the future.*
I hope cars will be cleaner.

1. _____

2. _____

3. _____

4. _____

5. _____

B. Interview. Choose one of the items in Activity A and interview a classmate.

Example: A: *Do you think airplanes will disappear completely?*
B: *No, I don't. But I think they will be different.*
A: *How will they be different?*
B: *I think they'll use nuclear power.*

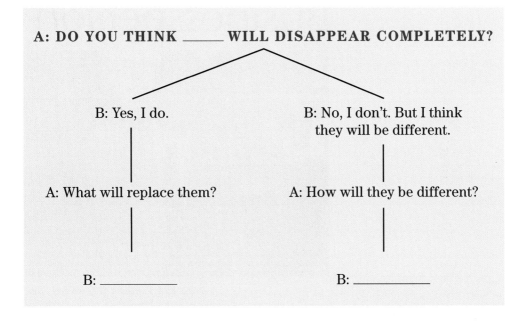

A: DO YOU THINK _____ WILL DISAPPEAR COMPLETELY?

B: Yes, I do.

A: What will replace them?

B: _____

B: No, I don't. But I think they will be different.

A: How will they be different?

B: _____

WORDS TO REMEMBER			
NOUNS	**VERBS**	**ADJECTIVES**	**ADVERBS**
computers	appear	a number of	entirely
experts	replace	cheaper	instantly
(the) Internet	preview	electronic	
inventions	press	likely	
technology		comfortable	
		convenient	
		permanent	
		similar (to)	

Chapter **4** How to Be a Successful Businessperson

Zubair Kazi, President of Kazi Foods, Inc.,
at a KFC restaurant he owns in Sylmar, California

*If at first you
don't succeed,
try, try again.*

—*American expression*

Before You Read

A. Look quickly over the article on pages 33–34 and complete this Previewing Chart.

PREVIEWING CHART	
Title of the article: _____	
Names of people and places in the article (List two more.)	**Key words** (What word appears several times? List three more.)
Zubair Kazi	restaurant
India	_____
_____	_____
_____	_____

B. Based on your chart, what do you think the story is about? Check (√) one or more ideas below.

I think this article is about someone who . . .

☐ is successful.   ☐ is from Canada.

☐ is a businessman.   ☐ owns a restaurant.

Reading Passage

HOW TO BE A SUCCESSFUL BUSINESSPERSON

1   Have you ever wondered[1] why some people are successful in business and others are not? Here's a story about one successful businessperson. He started out[2] washing dishes and today he owns 168 restaurants.

5   Zubair Kazi was born in Bhatkal, a small town in southwest **India.** His dream was to be an airplane pilot, and when he was 16 years old, he learned to fly a small plane.

At the age of 23 and with just a little money in his pocket, Mr. Kazi moved to the United States. He hoped to get a job in the airplane

---

[1] **wondered**   asked yourself
[2] **started out**   began his career

10   industry in California. Instead, he ended up working[3] for a company that rented cars.

While Mr. Kazi was working at the car rental company, he frequently ate at a nearby **KFC** restaurant. To save money on food,[4] he decided to get a job with KFC. For two months, he worked as a
15   cook's assistant. His job was to clean the kitchen and help the cook. "I didn't like it," Mr. Kazi says, "but I always did the best I could."[5]

One day, Mr. Kazi's two co-workers failed to come[6] to work. That day, Mr. Kazi did the work of all three people in the kitchen. This really impressed the owners[7] of the restaurant. A few months later,
20   the owners needed a manager for a new restaurant. They gave the job to Mr. Kazi. He worked hard as the manager and soon the restaurant was making a profit.[8]

A few years later, Mr. Kazi heard about a restaurant that was losing money. The restaurant was dirty inside and the food was terrible —
25   greasy[9] and undercooked. Mr. Kazi borrowed money from a bank and bought the restaurant. For the first six months, Mr. Kazi worked in the restaurant from 8 a.m. to 10 p.m., seven days a week. He and his wife cleaned up the restaurant, remodeled[10] the front of the building, and improved the cooking. They also tried hard to please the
30   customers. If someone had to wait more than ten minutes for their food, Mrs. Kazi gave them a free soda. Before long the restaurant was making a profit.

A year later Mr. Kazi sold his restaurant for a profit. With the money he earned, he bought three more restaurants that were losing money.
35   Again, he cleaned them up, improved the food, and retrained the employees. Before long[11] these restaurants were making a profit, too.

Today Mr. Kazi owns 168 restaurants, but he isn't planning to stop there. He's looking for more poorly managed restaurants to buy. "I love it when I go to buy a restaurant and find it's a mess," Mr. Kazi
40   says. "The only way it can go is up."[12]

This article was adapted from the Wall Street Journal.

---

[3] **he ended up working**   after much effort, he got a job

[4] **to save money on food**   to spend less money on food

[5] **did the best I could**   did the best job I could; worked as hard as I could

[6] **failed to come**   didn't come

[7] **impressed the owners**   made the owners think well of him

[8] **making a profit**   earning more money than it was spending

[9] **greasy**   with lots of oil; oily

[10] **remodeled**   fixed and painted

[11] **Before long**   after a short amount of time

[12] **the only way it can go is up**   it can only get better

After You Read

Understanding the Text

A. Sequence of events. Number these events in Mr. Kazi's life from 1 (the first) to 9 (the last).

_____ He sold his first restaurant at a profit.

_____ He got a job as a cook's helper.

__9__ He bought his 168th restaurant.

_____ He moved to the United States.

_____ He got a job at a car rental company.

__1__ He learned to fly a plane.

_____ He bought his first restaurant.

_____ He bought three more restaurants.

_____ He became the manager of a restaurant.

B. True or False. Read the statements below and check (√) True or False.

	True	False
1. Mr. Kazi moved to the United States because he wanted to be a restaurant manager.	☐	☐
2. He got a job in a restaurant because he wanted to save money on food.	☐	☐
3. His first restaurant job was as a cook's helper.	☐	☐
4. Mr. Kazi enjoyed working as a cook's helper.	☐	☐
5. To buy his first restaurant, Mr. Kazi borrowed money from his family.	☐	☐
6. Mr. Kazi was married while he owned his first restaurant.	☐	☐
7. The first restaurant Mr. Kazi bought was a mess.	☐	☐
8. Mr. Kazi lost money when he sold his first restaurant.	☐	☐

Work with a partner to correct the false statements.

C. Consider the issues. Work with a partner and follow the instructions below.

1. Choose an adjective that describes Mr. Kazi and complete the sentence below.

Adjectives

smart	hardworking	creative
serious	kind	successful

I think Mr. Kazi is a _____ *person.*

Now tell why you chose the word. Choose one or more reasons from the list below or think of your own.

Reasons

☐ because he moved to the U.S. with little money
☐ because he made a profit with his restaurants
☐ because he did the work of three people at KFC
☐ because he worked 7 days a week
☐ because he tried to please his customers
☐ because _____

Report your ideas to the class.

Example: *I think Mr. Kazi is a smart person because he made a profit with his restaurants.*

2. Group work. Think of a successful businessperson and answer the questions below. Don't tell the other groups the name of your person.

a. What did this person do?

b. How would you describe this person?

Example: *This person made one of the big car companies profitable. We think he is very smart.*

Read your answers to the class and let them guess the person.

Making inferences

An inference is a good guess or conclusion you can make from the facts you have.

Examples:

Fact	**Inference**
Mr. Kazi owns 168 restaurants. →	He's probably very busy. He has a lot of employees.

Fact	**Inference**
Mr. Kazi wanted a job in the airplane industry but he took a job with a car rental company. →	Mr. Kazi probably couldn't find a job in the airplane industry.

A. What inferences can you make about Mr. Kazi from the information below? Circle the best answer.

1. One day Mr. Kazi's two co-workers didn't come to work. That day, Mr. Kazi did the work of three people. From this information, you can say that . . .

a. Mr. Kazi probably worked very hard that day.

b. Mr. Kazi is probably a tall man.

c. Mr. Kazi probably didn't know his co-workers very well.

2. Mr. Kazi sold his first three restaurants for more money than he paid for them. From this information, you can say that . . .

a. Mr. Kazi is a good businessman.

b. Mr. Kazi is an honest man.

c. Mr. Kazi became a millionaire when he sold the restaurants.

B. What can you infer about Mr. Kazi from each statement below? Write your ideas.

1. Mr. Kazi started with very little money, but he now owns 168 restaurants.

You can infer that _____.

2. Mr. Kazi had very little money when he came to the United States.

You can infer that _____.

3. When the owners needed a manager for their new restaurant, they gave the job to Mr. Kazi.

You can infer that _____.

Making a word form chart

You can build your vocabulary by learning different forms of a word. For example, when you learn the adjective *successful*, you can also learn the noun *success*, the verb *succeed*, and the adverb *successfully*. (Not every word has four forms.)

In your vocabulary log, make a **Word Form Chart** like the one below.

Noun	Verb	Adjective	Adverb
success	succeed	successful	successfully
hope	hope	hopeful	hopefully
rent	rent	rental	
impression	impress	impressive	impressively
profit	profit	profitable	profitably
manager	manage	managerial	

A. Choose the correct form of the word in parentheses to complete each sentence.

1. (succeed / successful / successfully)

Mr. Kazi is a ___successful___ manager of 168 restaurants.

Mr. Kazi manages 168 restaurants _____ .

2. (rent / rented / rental)

For a while, Mr. Kazi worked at a car _____ company.

For a while, Mr. Kazi worked at a company that _____ cars.

3. (manager / managed / managerial)

Mr. Kazi was the _____ of a KFC restaurant.

Mr. Kazi _____ a KFC restaurant.

4. (impression / impressed / impressive)

Mr. Kazi's work _____ his employers.

Mr. Kazi's work made an _____ on his employers.

5. (profit / profited / profitable)

Mr. Kazi made a _____ from the sale of each restaurant.

Mr. Kazi _____ from the sale of each restaurant.

B. Choose six words from the article that you want to remember. Add them to your vocabulary log on page 170.

Using infinitives

Form: (to) + verb

to make, to see, to go, to travel

You can use an infinitive to:

- *identify something you hope, want, plan, or need to do.*
  Mr. Kazi hoped **to become** an airplane pilot.
  He wanted **to be** a pilot.

- *identify a plan, hope, dream*
  Mr. Kazi's dream was **to be** an airplane pilot.
  His plan was **to become** an airplane pilot.

- *identify a purpose for doing something*
  To please customers, Mr. Kazi gave them a free soda.
  To buy the restaurant, he borrowed money from the bank.

A. Choose a verb from the box to complete each sentence.

to buy	to fly	to please	to give
to come	to find	to save	to improve

1. When Mr. Kazi was 16, he learned _____ an airplane.

2. When he came to the United States, he hoped _____ a job in the airline industry.

3. _____ money on food, Mr. Kazi got a job at a restaurant.

4. One day his co-workers failed _____ to work.

5. The owners of the restaurant decided _____ Mr. Kazi the manager's job.

6. _____ their first restaurant, Mr. Kazi and his wife remodeled the front of the building and made the food better.

7. Mr. Kazi tried hard _____ the customers in his restaurant.

8. Mr. Kazi is planning _____ more restaurants.

B. Choose a verb from the box to complete each question. (More than one answer may be possible.)

to do	to fly	to ski	to study
to eat	to live	to travel	to make

1. What do you plan _____ this evening?
2. How are you planning _____ to Bali?
3. Where can you learn _____?
4. Have you ever tried _____?
5. Where would you like _____?
6. What do you hope _____ someday?
7. When do you want _____ for the test?
8. What are you planning _____ for dinner?
9. Have you ever forgotten _____ for a test?
10. Where do you hope _____ someday?

Ask a partner your questions.

Discussion & Writing

A. Group work. A manager supervises a group of employees. What do you think a good manager is like? Check (√) your answers below. Then add one or more of your own ideas.

IT'S IMPORTANT FOR A MANAGER TO	IT'S NOT IMPORTANT FOR A MANAGER TO	
☐	☐	be honest
☐	☐	be hardworking
☐	☐	be kind
☐	☐	make a profit
☐	☐	be able to make difficult decisions
☐	☐	communicate well

IT'S IMPORTANT FOR A MANAGER TO	IT'S NOT IMPORTANT FOR A MANAGER TO	
☐	☐	write well
☐	☐	treat the employees well
☐	☐	reduce stress in the workplace
☐	☐	listen to others
☐	☐	understand new technologies
☐	☐	hold parties for the employees

Share ideas with the other groups in your class.

Example: *We think it's important for a manager to be honest.*

B. Would you be a good manager? Complete one of the sentences below with information about yourself.

I think I would be a good manager because _____

_____

I don't think I would be a good manager because _____

_____

Share your ideas with a partner.

C. Pair work. Mr. Kazi tried hard to please his customers. What are some ways to please customers in each situation below? Add two ideas to each list.

WHAT COULD YOU DO TO PLEASE CUSTOMERS . . .		
IN A RESTAURANT?	**IN A DEPARTMENT STORE?**	**IN A BANK?**
give away free sodas	have good sales	provide good service
_____	_____	_____
_____	_____	_____

WORDS TO REMEMBER			
NOUNS	VERBS	ADJECTIVES	ADVERBS
businessperson	earn	successful	successfully
company	end up	impressive	(work) hard
dream	fail to	profitable	
job	hope		
manager	impress		
profit	improve		
success	succeed		
	lose (money)		
	own		
	save (money)		
	start out		
	wonder		

5 Tonic Water, Please

"What is he trying to say?"

"Why can't he understand me?"

Problems are messages.

—*Shakti Gawain, American author (1948–)*

Chapter Focus

CONTENT:
Communicating in a foreign language

READING SKILL:
Scanning

BUILDING VOCABULARY:
Understanding prefixes

LANGUAGE FOCUS:
Connecting ideas with *and*, *but*, and *however*

Before You Read

A. Look quickly over the story on pages 44–46 and complete the Previewing Chart below.

PREVIEWING CHART
Title of the article: _____

Names of people and places in the article (List three more.)	Key words (What word appears several times? List three more.)
Japan	English
_____	_____
_____	_____
_____	_____

B. Look at the picture on page 43. What do you think the story is about? Check (√) one or more ideas.

Example: *I think this story is about someone who . . .*

☐ is living in a foreign country.   ☐ owns a business.

☐ is lost.   ☐ is having trouble communicating.

☐ is angry.   ☐ has a problem.

Now read the story and check your guesses.

Reading Passage

TONIC WATER,[1] PLEASE

1   *Tetsuya Saruhashi grew up in Tokyo, Japan. He worked and studied for a year in Toronto, Canada. This story is based on two of Tetsuya's experiences there.*

How well do you speak English? Could you survive in an **English-**
5   **speaking country?** Last year I went to live and study in **Canada.** Before going, I took several English conversation classes. I also

---
[1] **tonic water**   a flavored water often used in alcoholic drinks

listened to a lot of English conversation tapes and I practiced speaking English with some foreign friends in my country. But could I communicate with people in Canada?

10   During my first months in Canada, I didn't have a lot of trouble understanding people. This was a happy surprise. Unfortunately, however, Canadians couldn't always understand me. This was because of my pronunciation.

My biggest pronunciation problems were with the "v" sound and
15   the "l" sound. For example, when I said the word *vote*, it sounded like *bote*. And when I said the word *late*, it sounded like *rate*. One day I decided to look for some **volunteer work**. I went to the **tourist center** in Toronto to ask for information about volunteering.

"Can I help you?" the woman at the tourist center asked.

20   "Yes, I'm looking for some volunteer work," I replied. Unfortunately, I pronounced the word "volunteer" like "borunteer."

"I'm sorry," she said, "What are you looking for?"

"Volunteer work," I answered, saying "borunteer" again. She looked at me strangely and then she called to a man behind the counter.

25   "Can I help you?" the man asked.

"Yes, I'm looking for some volunteer work," I repeated.

"Could you write that for me?" he asked. I wrote the words down and he immediately understood me. After that, I spent a lot of time practicing the *v* sound and the *l* sound.

30   I had trouble pronouncing a few other English sounds, too. I remember a funny experience I had at a **night club.** I wanted to get something to drink, so I went up to the **bartender.**

"Excuse me, tonic water, please," I said.

"What?" the bartender asked.

35   I asked, "Can I have a tonic water?"

"Say it again," he responded.

I was kind of[2] disappointed that he couldn't understand me. I repeated my request several times, but still he couldn't understand me. Then, suddenly, he opened the cash register[3] and took out some
40   **quarters.**[4] He put the quarters on the bar and began to count them. At first, I didn't know what he was doing. Then, suddenly, I

---

[2] **kind of**   (informal) a little

[3] **cash register**   a special machine where money is kept in a store or restaurant

[4] **quarters**   Canadian and U.S. coins worth twenty-five cents

understood. I asked for tonic water, but he thought I asked for
"twenty quarters"!

45   I burst into laughter[5] and said, "No, I didn't ask for twenty quarters.
I just want tonic water."

The bartender seemed embarrassed.[6] "I'm so sorry," he said to me.
"The music is so loud."

Now, whenever I ask for tonic water, I remember this incident and I
look forward to the bartender's response.

After You Read

Understanding the Text

A. **True or False?** Read the statements below and check (√) True or
False. Then write the number of the lines in the story that helped
you. The first one is done for you.

	True	False	Lines #
1. Tetsuya Saruhashi is from Japan.	☑	☐	1
2. He studied English before he traveled to Canada.	☐	☐	___
3. He lived for a year in Canada.	☐	☐	___
4. He couldn't understand English speakers when they talked to him.	☐	☐	___
5. Some Canadians couldn't understand Tetsuya when he spoke English.	☐	☐	___
6. Tetsuya had trouble pronouncing words with the "v" sound.	☐	☐	___
7. When the man at the tourist center couldn't understand him, Tetsuya spoke in Japanese.	☐	☐	___
8. Tetsuya asked the bartender at the night club for money.	☐	☐	___

Work with a partner to correct the false statements.

----

[5] **burst into laughter**   laughed very quickly and loudly

[6] **embarrassed**   ashamed or uncomfortable

B. Summarize. Read this summary and add the missing words.

Tetsuya Saruhashi is from _____ , but he lived and studied in Canada for a year. Before he went to Canada, he spent a lot of time studying E_____ . That's why he was able to u_____ people when he got to Canada. Unfortunately, however, many Canadians c_____ understand Tetsuya. This was because he had trouble p_____ some sounds in English. One time at a night club, Tetsuya ordered t_____ _____ , but the bartender thought he wanted _____ _____ . Tetsuya l_____ when he realized what the problem was.

C. Consider the issues. Follow the instructions below.

1. Rewrite one of the conversations in the story. Then read the new conversation with one or more classmates.

	PLACE	PEOPLE
Conversation #1	tourist center	Tetsuya female employee male employee
Conversation #2	night club	Tetsuya bartender

Example: *Conversation #1*
Woman: Can I help you?
Tetsuya: Yes, I'm looking for some "borunteer" work.
Woman: I'm sorry. What . . .

2. Pair work. What can you say when you don't understand someone? One person reads a question from Box A. The other person responds with a phrase from Box B. Then follow the example to finish the conversation. Practice both the formal and informal forms.

Example: *A: Where is Tetsuya from?*
B: Excuse me?
A: Where is Tetsuya from?
B: Japan. He's from Japan.

Box A

- Where is Tetsuya from?
- What is tonic water?
- Where is Toronto?
- Do you like pizza?
- Have you ever done volunteer work?

Box B
Formal
Excuse me?
Could you repeat that?
Could you say that again?
Could you write that for me?

Informal
Say it again.
What?
What did you say?

3. What pronunciation problems do foreigners have when they speak your language? Think of one or more examples.

Examples:

Foreigners sometimes say _____ instead of _____.

Some foreigners can't pronounce the sound _____.

Reading Skill

Scanning

When you need to find specific information in a text, you don't have to read every word. Instead, you can move your eyes quickly over the text to find the information. This is called **scanning.**

A. Scanning. Read the questions below. Then scan (don't read) the following paragraph to find the answers.

QUESTIONS	
1. What city is this paragraph about?	_____
2. What is the population of the city?	_____
3. Is there information about the food in this country?	YES NO
4. Is there information about the schools in this country?	YES NO

Taipei

Taipei is a lively and expensive city, and it lets you know it. About 6,000,000 people live in and around the capital of Taiwan and it is a hotbed of *renao*, or liveliness. Apartments are almost impossible to buy in Taipei and the government is encouraging businesses to locate in other parts of the country. Taipei may not be a relaxing place but the food is excellent, the people are friendly, and there are some wonderful things to see, like the Grand Hotel.

B. Making inferences. What inferences can you make from statements below? Circle the letter of your answers.

Example: *"Apartments are almost impossible to buy in Taipei and the government is encouraging businesses to locate in other parts of the country."*

    a. It's easier to buy an apartment outside of Taipei.
    b. There aren't many apartments in Taipei.
    c. There aren't many people in Taipei.

1. "During Tetsuya's first months in Canada, he didn't have a lot of trouble understanding people. This was a happy surprise for him."

    a. Tetsuya expected to have trouble understanding people in Canada.

    b. Tetsuya didn't expect to have trouble understanding people in Canada.

    c. After a few months, Tetsuya had trouble understanding Canadians.

2. "One day I decided to look for some volunteer work."

    a. He needed some money.

    b. He is very rich.

    c. He could afford to work for free.

3. "Excuse me, tonic water, please," Tetsuya said.
"What?" the bartender asked.
"Can I have a tonic water?" Tetsuya asked again.
"Say it again," he responded.

   a. The bartender was angry.

   b. The bartender didn't have any tonic water.

   c. The bartender couldn't understand Tetsuya.

Building Vocabulary

Understanding Prefixes

You can add the prefix *mis-* to the beginning of certain words. This adds the meaning *incorrectly* or *badly*. For example, the word *mispronounce* means *to pronounce* (something) *incorrectly*. Here are some other words to which you can add the prefix *mis-*:

count	⟶	miscount
inform	⟶	misinform
manage	⟶	mismanage
pronounce	⟶	mispronounce
read	⟶	misread
spell	⟶	misspell
understand	⟶	misunderstand

A. Choose a verb from the box above to complete each sentence. Use the correct form of the verb.

   1. I couldn't understand him because he _____ the word *volunteer*.

   2. I _____ the directions and got lost.

   3. If you _____ my name, I won't get your email message.

   4. Read the instructions carefully so that you don't _____ them.

   5. The people at the tourist center _____ me. They told me the bus left at nine, but it left at ten.

   6. The new owners _____ the company and it lost a lot of money.

7. I _____ my money. I thought I had ten Canadian dollars but I only had nine.

8. John _____ me. I asked him to buy eight cans of tonic water, but he bought eighteen.

9. I _____ the train schedule. I thought it left at three o'clock, but it left at eight o'clock.

B. Choose six words from the reading that you want to remember. Add them to your vocabulary log on page 171.

Language Focus

Connecting ideas with <u>and</u>, <u>but</u>, and <u>however</u>
We use the word *and* to connect ideas that are similar.

- I understand most people, **and** they understand me.

We use the words *but* and *however* to connect ideas that are different in some way. *However* usually comes after a semicolon.

- I understand most people, **but** they don't understand me.

- I didn't have trouble understanding people; **however,** they had trouble understanding me.

A. Complete each pair of sentences with **and**, **but**, or **however**.

1. **a.** I have many Canadian friends; _____, we never speak English together. We speak French.

   b. I have many Canadian friends, _____ I often practice speaking English with them.

2. **a.** I asked for information, _____ she was able to help me.

   b. I asked for information, _____ she couldn't help me.

3. **a.** I like to listen to English tapes; _____, I rarely practice speaking English with foreigners here.

   b. I like to listen to English tapes, _____ I often practice speaking English with foreigners here.

B. What happened? Read each conversation and complete the summary statement. Use **and**, **but**, or **however**.

1. Tina: Would you like some coffee?
Tetsuya: I'm sorry. What did you say?

Summary statement: Tina offered Tetsuya some coffee, _____ he didn't understand her.

2. Tetsuya: Do you want to go for coffee?
Tina: Sure, I'd love to.

Summary statement: Tetsuya invited Tina to go for coffee, _____ she said she'd love to.

3. Tina: Is Tetsuya there?
Ken: No, I'm sorry, he's not. Can I take a message?

Summary statement: Tina called Tetsuya on the telephone; _____ , he wasn't there.

Discussion & Writing

A. Do you think it's easy or difficult to do these things in a foreign country? Check (√) your answers. Then share your work with classmates. Add two ideas of your own.

		I THINK IT WOULD BE . . .
EASY	DIFFICULT	
☐	☐	to meet people
☐	☐	to make new friends
☐	☐	to understand people
☐	☐	to communicate my ideas
☐	☐	to order food in a restaurant
☐	☐	to learn to use the subway
☐	☐	to answer questions about my country
☐	☐	_____
☐	☐	_____

B. Think of an experience you had talking to someone from another country and answer the questions below.

1. Where were you?

2. What did you talk about?

3. Did you have any communication problems?

4. How did you solve these problems?

Now write a short description of your experience.

Example:

○	One time a foreigner stopped me on the street. She was lost, and she wanted directions. Her pronunciation was pretty good, so I thought she could speak my language. When I gave her the directions, however, she didn't understand me at all. I ended up walking with her to her destination.	

WORDS TO REMEMBER			
NOUNS	**VERBS**	**ADJECTIVES**	**ADVERBS**
experience	communicate	disappointed	strangely
response	have (trouble)	embarrassed	unfortunately
volunteer work	pronounce		
	respond		
	volunteers		
	practice		

Chapter **6** Cell Phones: Hang Up or Keep Talking?

▲

Students outside a dormitory at Salem State College,
Salem, Massachusetts, USA

Look before you leap.¹

—*English expression*

Chapter Focus

▼

CONTENT:
The dangers of cell phone use

READING SKILL:
Understanding the difference between
facts and opinions

BUILDING VOCABULARY:
Expressing certainty and uncertainty

LANGUAGE FOCUS:
Understanding what pronouns refer to

¹ **leap** jump

Before You Read

A. Scan the article on pages 55–56 and complete the Previewing Chart below.

<table>
<tr><td colspan="2">PREVIEWING CHART</td></tr>
<tr><td colspan="2">Title of the article:_____</td></tr>
<tr><td>Names of professions and
places in the article
(List three more.)
health professionals</td><td>Key words (What word
appears several times?
List three more.)
worried</td></tr>
</table>

B. Based on the chart above, what do you think the article is about? Check (√) one or more ideas.

    Example: *I think this article is about . . .*

    ☐ communication problems

    ☐ the possible dangers of cell phones

    ☐ why people use cell phones

    ☐ the future of cell phones

    ☐ _____

Reading Passage

CELL PHONES: HANG UP² OR KEEP TALKING?

1   Millions of people are using cell phones today. In many places it is actually considered unusual not to use one. In many countries, cell phones are very popular with young people. They find that the phones are more than a means of communication — having a mobile
5 phone³ shows that they are cool⁴ and connected.

---

² **hang up** turn the telephone off
³ **mobile phone** cell phone
⁴ **cool** doing things that are popular

The explosion[5] around the world in mobile phone use[6] has some **health professionals** worried. Some doctors are concerned that in the future many people may suffer health problems[7] from the use of mobile phones. In England, there has been a serious debate about
10 this issue. Mobile phone companies are worried about the **negative publicity** of such ideas. They say that there is no proof[8] that mobile phones are bad for your health.

On the other hand, why do some medical studies show changes in the brain cells of some people who use mobile phones? Signs
15 of change in the tissues of the brain and head can be detected[9] with modern scanning equipment.[10] In one case, a **traveling salesman** had to retire[11] at a young age because of serious memory loss. He couldn't remember even simple tasks.[12] He would often forget the name of his own son. This man used to talk on his mobile phone for
20 about six hours a day, every day of his working week, for a couple of years. His family doctor blamed his mobile phone use,[13] but his employer's doctor didn't agree.

What is it that makes mobile phones potentially harmful? The answer is **radiation.** High-tech[14] machines can detect very small
25 amounts of radiation from mobile phones. Mobile phone companies agree that there is some radiation, but they say the amount is too small to worry about.

As the discussion about their safety continues, it appears that it's best to use mobile phones less often. Use your regular phone if you
30 want to talk for a long time. Use your mobile phone only when you really need it. Mobile phones can be very useful and convenient, especially in emergencies. In the future, mobile phones may have a **warning label** that says they are bad for your health. So for now, it's wise not to use your mobile phone too often.

---

[5] **explosion**   sudden increase

[6] **mobile phone use**   the number of people using mobile phones

[7] **suffer health problems (from)**   have health problems caused by

[8] **there is no proof (that)**   there are no facts to show that; there is no evidence that

[9] **detected**   seen; found

[10] **modern scanning equipment**   new medical machines showing things inside the body

[11] **retire**   stop working

[12] **tasks**   jobs; things to do

[13] **blamed his mobile phone use**   said that using his mobile phone caused the problem

[14] **high–tech**   advanced technology

After You Read

Understanding the Text

A. Multiple choice. For each item below, circle the best answer.

1. This article is about _____.

   a. the possible dangers of mobile phone use

   b. why mobile phones are popular

   c. how mobile phones work

2. The writer's purpose in writing this article was to _____.

   a. convince people that cell phones may be dangerous

   b. convince people that cell phones are dangerous

   c. convince people to buy cell phones

3. Paragraph 4 (lines 23–27) is about _____.

   a. the increase in mobile phone use

   b. what makes mobile phones potentially dangerous

   c. how to avoid the possible dangers of mobile phones

4. Another word for *means* in line 4 is _____.

   a. unkind

   b. method

   c. expression

5. In line 23, the word *potentially* means _____.

   a. certainly

   b. possibly

   c. privately

6. You can infer from the information in paragraph 2 (lines 6–12) that mobile phone companies _____.

   a. know that cell phones are dangerous to your health

   b. have proof that cell phones are not dangerous to your health

   c. are afraid that information about cell phone health problems will hurt their business

B. Consider the issues. Work with a partner to answer the questions below.

1. What are the advantages and disadvantages of cell phones? Write each sentence from the box below under "Advantages" or "Disadvantages." Then add one more of your own.

CELL PHONES
• They are easy to carry.
• They are small.
• They sometimes ring during concerts and movies.
• They are expensive.
• It's easy to lose them.
• You can talk on the phone anywhere.
• Cell phone users have more car accidents.

ADVANTAGES OF CELL PHONES	DISADVANTAGES OF CELL PHONES
They are easy to carry.	_____
_____	_____
_____	_____
_____	_____

2. **Pair work.** Write five sentences comparing mobile phones with regular phones. Use the adjectives in the box.

Comparative Forms of Adjectives	
cheaper	more convenient
smaller	more popular
safer	more comfortable
easier to lose	_____

Example: *Regular phones are cheaper than mobile phones.*

1. _____
2. _____
3. _____
4. _____
5. _____

Understanding the difference between facts and opinions

When you read, it's important to know the difference between facts and opinions. A fact is something you know is true. With a fact, there is information to show it is true. An opinion is something you *think* is true. An opinion is based on feelings, not facts.

Fact: Mobile phones send out small amounts of radiation.
Opinion: Using a mobile phone makes you look cool.

Fact or Opinion? Read the statements and check (√) Fact or Opinion.

	Fact	Opinion
1. Millions of people use mobile phones today.	☐	☐
2. In the future, many people may suffer health problems from the use of cell phones.	☐	☐
3. High-tech machines can detect very small amounts of radiation from mobile phones.	☐	☐
4. The amount of radiation from cell phones is very small.	☐	☐
5. Cell phones aren't dangerous because the amount of radiation from them is very small.	☐	☐
6. There are more cell phone users today than in 1995.	☐	☐
7. Many Asian students study in England and the United States every year.	☐	☐
8. In the future people won't read as many books as they do today.	☐	☐
9. Mr. Kazi is a successful businessperson.	☐	☐
10. There is a hotel called the Grand Hotel in Taipei, Taiwan.	☐	☐

Compare your answers with a partner.

Expressing certainty and uncertainty

Writers use different expressions to tell if they are certain or uncertain about something.

Examples:
Uncertain: It appears that it's dangerous to use cell phones.
Certain: It's a fact that mobile phones give out some radiation.

Certain		Uncertain
It's a fact that	I'm certain that	It appears that
It's certain that	I'm positive that	It seems that
It's true that	I'm sure that	It's possible that
Studies show that	I know that	I think that
		The research indicates that

A. Complete each sentence with a phrase from the box above. More than one answer is possible.

1. _____ mobile phones cause cancer.

2. _____ the sun causes cancer.

3. _____ there has been an explosion in mobile phone use.

4. _____ mobile phones will become more popular in the future.

5. _____ large amounts of radiation are dangerous.

B. Pair work. For each topic below, complete the sentences. (Many different answers are possible.)

1. Topic: cell phones
   a. It's possible that *cell phones are dangerous to your health.*
   b. It's a fact that _____

2. Topic: studying abroad
   a. It seems that _____
   b. I'm certain that _____

3. Topic: sleep
   a. It's possible that _____
   b. Studies show that _____

4. Topic: books

    a. I think that _____

    b. It's a fact that _____

C. Choose six words from the reading that you want to remember. Add them to your vocabulary log on page 171.

Language Focus

Understanding what pronouns refer to

We often use a pronoun instead of repeating the name of a person, place, or thing. When you read, it's important to know what a pronoun refers to. In the example below, the pronoun *they* refers to "young people in many parts of the world."

Example:

In many parts of the world, mobile phones are very popular with young people. **They** find that the phones are more than a means of communication — having a cell phone shows that **they** are cool and connected.

A. Read these sentences. Then write what each underlined pronoun refers to.

1. Mobile phone companies agree that there is some radiation, but they say the amount of radiation is too small to worry about.

In this sentence, the pronoun "they" refers to _____.

2. There have been some concerns about long-term use of a mobile phone and the effect it might have on the human body.

In this sentence, the pronoun "it" refers to _____.

3. Some health professionals are worried about the explosion in mobile phone use. They are concerned that people may suffer health problems in the future.

In this sentence, the pronoun "they" refers to _____.

4. Radiation is potentially harmful and high-tech machines can detect small amounts of it coming from mobile phones.

In this sentence, the pronoun "it" refers to _____.

5. In the future, mobile phones may have a warning label attached that says they are bad for your health.

In this sentence, the pronoun "they" refers to _____.

B. Rewrite each sentence. Replace the underlined words with a pronoun.

1. A Danish study of cell phone users did not prove that <u>cell phone users</u> are more likely to get cancer.

   A Danish study of cell phone users did not prove that they are

   more likely to get cancer.

2. The radiation in laboratory tests may not have penetrated the cells as <u>radiation</u> would penetrate the brain in real life.

   _____

   _____

3. Scientists are eagerly awaiting the results of a very large study of cell phone users in Europe. Unfortunately, <u>the study</u> won't be available for several more years.

   _____

   _____

4. Many of my Japanese classmates didn't use their English very much even though <u>many of my Japanese classmates</u> had large vocabularies.

   _____

   _____

5. A few years ago, it seemed likely that computers would replace books. Now, however, most experts think <u>books</u> are here to stay.

   _____

   _____

6. Mr. Kazi's job was to clean the kitchen. "I didn't like <u>the job</u>," Mr. Kazi says, "but I always did the best I could."

   _____

   _____

A. What looks "cool" to you? Check (√) your answers.

I THINK	I DON'T THINK _____ LOOKS COOL.	
☐	☐	talking on a cell phone
☐	☐	wearing high-heeled shoes
☐	☐	wearing lots of jewelry
☐	☐	wearing boots
☐	☐	wearing headphones
☐	☐	smoking cigarettes
☐	☐	driving a sports car
☐	☐	tattoos
☐	☐	nose rings
☐	☐	_____

B. Pair work. One person identifies something that looks cool. The other person agrees or disagrees.

Example: A: *I think talking on a cell phone looks cool.*
              B: *Interesting. I think wearing a lot of jewelry looks cool.*
              A: *So do I. And I think . . .*

A: I think _____ looks cool.

(Agree)
B: So do I. And I think _____ looks cool too.

(Disagree)
B: Interesting. I think _____ looks cool.

C. Pair work. The writer of the article on pages 55–56 suggests that people use cell phones sensibly or wisely. Write a list of "dos" and "don'ts" for using a cell phone wisely.

USING A CELL PHONE WISELY	
DO	**DON'T**
• *speak softly*	• _____
• _____	• _____
• _____	• _____

Compare your lists with another pair of students.

WORDS TO REMEMBER			
NOUNS	**VERBS**	**ADJECTIVES**	**ADVERBS**
amount	agree	concerned	softly
danger	blame	convenient	wisely
health	retire	harmful	potentially
radiation	suffer	popular	
use	use	unusual	
means		wise	
		cool	

Chapter

7

▲

The Ghost Pilot

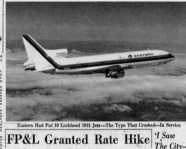

The Miami Herald

Partly Cloudy ... Saturday, December 30, 1972 ... *Florida's Complete Newspaper* ... **Final** 10 Cents ... 76 Pages

N.Y.-to-Miami Plane Crashes In Everglades With 167 Aboard

Is Razing Of Hanoi U.S. Aim?

Eastern Had Put 10 Lockheed 1011 Jets—The Type That Crashed—In Service

FP&L Granted Rate Hike

Eastern Jet Left Kennedy

Hospitals Report Some Survivors

'I Saw The City-- And Bang

Seeing is believing.

—*English expression*

Chapter Focus

CONTENT:
A ghost story

READING SKILL:
Summarizing

BUILDING VOCABULARY:
Learning synonyms

LANGUAGE FOCUS:
Using *must have* + past participle

Before You Read

A. Scan the story on pages 67–68 and complete the chart below.

<table>
<tr><th colspan="2">PREVIEWING CHART</th></tr>
<tr><td colspan="2">Title of the article: _____</td></tr>
<tr>
<td>Names of people and places in the article
(List three more.)

Florida _____

_____

_____

_____</td>
<td>Key words (What word appears several times? List three more.)

captain _____

_____

_____

_____</td>
</tr>
<tr><td colspan="2">I think this story is about: _____</td></tr>
</table>

B. Several strange things happen in the story on pages 67–68. Read the story and take notes in the chart below.

WHAT HAPPENED?	WHERE DID IT HAPPEN?	WHEN DID IT HAPPEN?
Flight 401 crashed	in the Everglades	on December 12, 1972
_____	in the first-class section of an Eastern Airlines plane	in March 1973
_____ _____	in the staff room at John F. Kennedy airport	in March 1973
_____ _____	in the first-class section of an Eastern Airlines plane	in April 1973

THE GHOST[1] PILOT

1   Just before midnight on December 12, 1972, Eastern Airlines Flight
       401 fell out of the sky.[2] The airplane crashed in the **Everglades** area
       of Florida. Of the 176 people on board,[3] 99 died, including the
       airplane's pilot, Bob Loft, and the flight engineer, Don Repo.

5   About three months after the crash, a high-ranking executive[4] of
       Eastern Airlines boarded an aircraft for Miami, Florida. He spotted a
       man in a pilot's uniform sitting alone in the **first-class section** and
       went to sit down beside him. The executive struck up a conversation[5]
       with the captain. After a few minutes he realized that he was talking to
10   the pilot Bob Loft. Then the pilot faded away.[6]

       A week later, an Eastern Airlines pilot and two of his crew went into
       a staff room[7] at John F. Kennedy Airport, in New York. They all saw
       Bob Loft in a chair. He talked to them for a while, then vanished. The
       men were so shocked[8] that the airline had to cancel[9] their flight.

15   Three weeks later, a passenger was sitting in the first-class section
       of a flight to Miami. She was worried about the man in an Eastern
       Airlines uniform sitting next to her. His face was white and he looked
       ill, so she called the **flight attendant.**

       The flight attendant leaned down to speak to the man but he
20   ignored her.[10] Then, as she touched his arm, he slowly faded away,
       leaving only an empty seat.

       When the plane landed in Miami, the passenger was taken to a
       hospital in a state of shock. Later, when she saw photographs, she
       identified the ghost as flight engineer Don Repo.

25   Over the next few months, more than ten flight attendants claimed
       to see Don Repo. The ghost seemed to appear more often on some

---

[1] **ghost**   the spirit of a dead person
[2] **fell out of the sky**   fell to the ground; crashed
[3] **on board**   on the airplane
[4] **a high-ranking executive**   an important person in the company
[5] **struck up a conversation**   started a conversation
[6] **faded away**   slowly disappeared
[7] **staff room**   a room for workers, but not customers
[8] **shocked**   very surprised
[9] **cancel**   stop
[10] **ignored her**   pretended she wasn't there

aircraft[11] than on others. Rumors began to spread[12] that he appeared only on planes with replacement parts from the crashed Flight 401. It was usual practice for an airline to use undamaged parts from a crashed plane in another plane if they passed strict[13] **safety tests.**

30

The stories must have worried the bosses of Eastern Airlines. They ordered their engineers to remove from their planes all equipment from the 401 wreck.[14]

It seemed to work. When all of the parts from Flight 401 had been removed, Bob Loft and Don Repo left Eastern Airlines and their aircraft in peace.[15] No one has seen their ghosts since.

35

After You Read

Understanding the Text

A. True or False? Read the statements and check (√) True or False.

	True	False
1. Don Repo and Bob Loft died in an airplane crash.	☐	☐
2. We don't know why Flight 401 crashed.	☐	☐
3. The ghost of Don Repo appeared on all Eastern Airlines flights.	☐	☐
4. More than one person saw the ghost of Bob Loft.	☐	☐
5. All of the people who saw the ghost of Don Repo and Bob Loft were airline employees.	☐	☐
6. The word *spotted* in line 6 means *talked to.*	☐	☐
7. The word *vanished* in line 13 means *disappeared.*	☐	☐
8. You can infer that Flight 401 was probably using undamaged parts from another aircraft.	☐	☐

Work with a partner to correct the false statements.

---

[11] **aircraft**   airplanes
[12] **rumors began to spread**   people started saying
[13] **strict**   difficult and demanding
[14] **the 401 wreck**   the crashed plane (Flight 401)
[15] **left the aircraft in peace**   didn't bother the aircraft again

B. Summarize. Read this summary of "The Ghost Pilot" and add the missing words.

Summary

The Ghost Pilot is a story about some strange things that happened after Flight 401 c_____ in 1972. Several months after the accident, a number of people saw Bob Loft and Don Repo, the pilot and flight engineer of Flight 401 who d_____ in the crash. For example, an airline executive saw Bob Loft in the first-class s_____ of an airplane. An airplane pilot saw Bob Loft in an airport s_____. Some people thought the two ghosts appeared only on flights with r_____ parts from the crashed Flight 401. After the engineers r_____ the replacement parts, Bob Loft and Don Repo stopped appearing.

C. Consider the issues. Work with a partner to answer the questions below.

1. Which parts of the story seem possible to you? Which parts don't seem possible? Add two more ideas to the chart below.

IT SEEMS POSSIBLE THAT . . .	IT DOESN'T SEEM POSSIBLE THAT . . .
a. the executive of Eastern Airlines had a conversation with a pilot.	a. the pilot faded away while the executive was talking to him.
b.	b.
c.	c.

2. According to the story, airlines can use undamaged parts from a crashed plane. What is one advantage and one disadvantage of doing this?

One advantage is that _____

One disadvantage is that _____

3. The quotation on page 65 reads "Seeing is believing." What does this mean? How does it relate to the story?

Reading Skill

Summarizing

When you summarize, you retell the most important information in your own words. Summarizing something you read can help you remember information.

Summary of paragraph #1, page 67:
Eastern Airlines Flight 401 crashed in Florida in 1972. More than half of the people on the flight died.

A. Complete these summaries. (More than one answer may be possible.)

1. Summary of paragraph #2 (lines 5–10):

A few months after the accident, an airline ___*executive*___ was traveling in an airplane to _____. After talking to another passenger for awhile, he realized the person was _____. Then the person _____.

2. Summary of paragraph #3 (lines 11–14):

Three airline employees thought they talked to Bob Loft in an airport _____. They were so upset, the airlines had to _____ their flight.

3. Summary of paragraphs #4 to #6 (lines 15–24).

One passenger was worried because the man next to her looked _____. Then, when a flight attendant touched the man, he _____. The passenger later identified the man as _____.

Learning synonyms

Synonyms are words that are similar in meaning. The verbs *leave* and *depart* are synonyms. So are the verbs *order* and *demand*.

Good writers often use synonyms to avoid repeating a word in a paragraph or story. In the story on pages 67–68, the writer used the synonyms *faded away* and *vanished*.

A. Three of the words in each group are synonyms. Cross out the word that is **not** a synonym.

    Example: *sick* ~~*happy*~~ *unwell* *ill*

1. feel   notice   see   spot
2. disappear   fade away   shock   vanish
3. concerned   unexpected   troubled   worried
4. ask   answer   respond   reply
5. claimed   said   stated   repeated
6. regular   normal   serious   usual
7. depart   join   leave   take off
8. dangerous   harmful   unsafe   convenient
9. fail   dream   hope   plan

Compare your answers with a partner.

B. Pair work. Look back at the reading to find synonyms for these words.

1. In line 7, find a synonym for *area*. _____
2. In line 10, find a synonym for *disappeared*. _____
3. In line 12, find a synonym for *spotted*. _____
4. In line 17, find a synonym for *seemed*. _____
5. In line 22, find a synonym for *arrived*. _____
6. In line 29, find a synonym for *common*. _____
7. In line 31, find a synonym for *executives*. _____

C. Choose six words from the reading that you want to remember. Add them to your vocabulary log on page 172.

Using **must have** + past participle

We often use *must have* + past participle to make a conclusion about something that happened in the past.

Example:

The stories *must have worried* the bosses of Eastern Airlines. They ordered their engineers to remove equipment from the 401 wreck.

A. Circle the word that best completes each sentence.

1. The flight attendant must have been (shocked/happy) when she touched the man's arm and he disappeared.

2. The pilot must have felt (okay/sick) if he wasn't able to fly the airplane.

3. The woman must have looked at the man (carefully/quickly) because she was able to identify him later from a photograph.

4. If they used a part from Flight 401 on another aircraft, the part must have (failed/passed) the safety test.

B. Match an item from Column A with one from Column B to complete each sentence.

1. If they took her to the hospital, she

2. If she couldn't sleep all night, she

3. If there isn't any food in the house, he

4. If the door is locked, they

5. If he did well on the test, he

6. If you can't hear the radio, she

7. If they didn't call, they

8. If he bought a car, he

_____ must have gone away.

_____ must have studied.

_____ must have turned it off.

_____ must not have gone to the supermarket.

_____ must have lost your number.

_____ must have felt tired the next day.

_____ must have borrowed money from the bank.

__1__ must have been really sick.

Compare answers with your classmates.

A. Think of an accident that you have heard or read about. Write about your memories of the accident in the chart below. Use the question words to organize your story.

Who Who was in the accident?	
Where Where did the accident happen?	
When When did the accident happen?	
What What caused the accident? What happened?	

Use your chart to tell your classmates about the accident.

B. Group work. Follow the steps below to play the game Two Truths and One Lie.

Step 1: Write two true things and one untrue thing about yourself.

Examples:	I have never eaten a hamburger.
	I broke my leg five years ago.
	I think sailing is a lot of fun.
Hint:	Make it difficult for your classmates to guess the untrue sentence.

Step 2: Read the three statements to your classmates. Ask them to identify the false statement.

IDENTIFY TRUE AND FALSE STATEMENTS

- I think it's true that . . . _____
- It's hard to believe that . . . _____
- I can't believe that . . . _____

C. Ghost stories are popular in many countries. Even though these stories are about very strange things, many people believe them. Why do you think people believe ghost stories?

I think people believe ghost stories because . . .

WORDS TO REMEMBER

NOUNS	VERBS	ADJECTIVES
aircraft	crash	empty
flight attendant	die	ill
passenger	ignore	shocked
pilot	land	strict
	remove	usual
	spot	
	vanish	

Chapter ▲

8 Helping Others

Mariko Asano, a Habitat for Humanity volunteer,
helps build a house in the Philippines.

*When one helps
another, both gain
in strength.*

—*South American proverb*

Chapter Focus ▼

CONTENT:
Volunteering

READING SKILL:
Identifying the topic and main idea

BUILDING VOCABULARY:
Using prefixes: *un-, im-, in-, ir-*

LANGUAGE FOCUS:
Understanding gerunds

Before You Read

Read these dictionary definitions and answer the questions below.

> **volunteer** *noun* a person who offers or agrees to do something without being forced or paid to do it: *He does a lot of volunteer work at the hospital.*
>
> **volunteer** *verb* to offer to do something which you do not have to do or for which you will not be paid: *She volunteered for the school's social committee.*

A. Think of something you volunteered to do for a friend, family member, or organization. Who did you help? What did you do?

B. Think of two more volunteer organizations and complete the chart.

NAME OF VOLUNTEER ORGANIZATION	PURPOSE
1. The International Red Cross	to help people after disasters
2.	
3.	

C. Read the introduction to the article on page 76–77. Add information about the volunteer organization Habitat for Humanity to the chart above. What do you think the reading will be about?

Reading Passage

HELPING OTHERS

by Mariko Asano

Introduction

Habitat for Humanity International—or Habitat—is a nonprofit organization that helps people in need[1] build houses. Since 1976, volunteers for Habitat have built more than 100,000 houses worldwide. According to Habitat, however, there are still more than 1.5 billion people in the world without

---

[1] **in need** who need help

decent housing.[2] *In the article below, Mariko Asano talks about her experience as a Habitat* **volunteer.** *She has traveled to the* **Philippines** *three times to help build houses for people who need them.*

1   I am 24 years old and I grew up in **Nishinomiya, Japan.** Several years ago, I went to **Negros Island** in the Philippines as a Habitat volunteer. This was the first of three trips I have taken to the Philippines as a volunteer. For me, the idea of building somebody's 5 house abroad was very exciting. The next year I returned to Negros Island as a Habitat volunteer. This time I went as a student leader with 28 classmates from Kyoto University of Foreign Studies.

     Both the staff[3] and the families on Negros Island became dear friends of the work team I led.[4] Meeting these people was wonderful 10 for each of us. Their lifestyle reminded us of the meaning and value of life. The people also helped us appreciate the more valuable things in life, such as spending time with your family, friends and neighbors; developing close relationships; helping each other; and appreciating[5] what you do have. These things are sometimes forgotten in an 15 affluent country[6] like Japan.

     We thought we came to the Philippines to help the Filipino people, but they helped us to see something valuable. They generously offered their food, space, and hearts[7] in a way we were not accustomed to. (Would you give up your bed for a stranger and sleep 20 on the cement floor at your own house?)

     When I took my third trip to the Philippines as a Habitat volunteer, I was assigned to[8] a house with young people from around the world. In my group, there were Filipinos, Americans, Indians, Koreans, and Japanese. We worked together to complete a house for a family we 25 met on the site.[9] On the last day, all of us stood inside a room we had built in just a week, feeling a sense of fulfillment.[10] Even now we keep

---

[2] **decent housing**   housing of an acceptable standard; livable housing

[3] **staff**   employees

[4] **the work team I led**   group of workers I was responsible for

[5] **appreciating**   being thankful for

[6] **an affluent country**   a wealthy country

[7] **offered their food, space, and hearts**   gave us food, a place to stay, and kindness

[8] **was assigned to**   was sent to work in; was given a job in

[9] **on the site**   at the place (where they built the house)

[10] **a sense of fulfillment**   a feeling of accomplishment

in touch across the world. Some of us are actively involved in Habitat in different countries.

30   Habitat brings people together and helps us realize that people all over the world care about each other. Habitat sends the very important message that we can all be friends. Being involved with Habitat for Humanity has changed my life. I've learned that I can make a difference[11] in the world.

After You Read

Understanding the Text

A. **Multiple choice.** For each item below, circle the best answer.

1. The writer's purpose in writing the article was to _____.

   a. convince people to travel

   b. discourage people from giving money for housing

   c. share a valuable experience about volunteering

2. Which statement is true?

   a. Habitat for Humanity is more than 25 years old.

   b. The writer is an employee of Habitat for Humanity.

   c. The writer has helped to build houses in more than one country.

3. In line 1, the words *grew up* mean _____.

   a. studied

   b. became tall

   c. spent my childhood

4. In lines 26–27, the words *keep in touch* mean _____.

   a. communicate

   b. make money

   c. walk

5. You can infer from paragraph #1 (lines 1–7) that Mariko Asano _____.

   a. is still a student at Kyoto University of Foreign Studies

   b. studied at Kyoto University of Foreign Studies

   c. was a teacher at Kyoto University of Foreign Studies

---

[11] **make a difference**   do something important for other people

6. You can infer from paragraph #4 (lines 21–28) that Mariko Asano
_____ .

    a. knew the family before she went to the Philippines

    b. didn't finish building the house

    c. was happy with the house her team built

B. Consider the issues. Work with a partner to answer the questions below.

  1. Pair work. In paragraph #2 (lines 8–15), what does Mariko Asano say are the valuable things in life? List four things below.

Valuable Things in Life

- _____
- _____
- _____
- _____

Choose one of Mariko's ideas and complete the sentence below.

Example: *We think it's important to help each other because together we are stronger.*

            We think it's important to _____ because . . .

  2. In your opinion, what are some of the positive and negative things about volunteering for Habitat? Add four ideas to the chart below.

POSITIVE THINGS	NEGATIVE THINGS
1. You can help other people.	1. You don't earn any money.
2. _____	2. _____
3. _____	3. _____

Based on the information in your chart, would you encourage someone to volunteer for Habitat? Why or why not?

Identifying the topic and main idea
To identify the **topic** of a reading, ask: *What is the reading about?*
To identify the **main idea** of a reading, ask: *What is the most important thing the writer says about the topic?*

Example:
The **topic** of the reading on pages 77–78 is volunteering for Habitat. The writer's **main idea** is that volunteering to help other people can change your life.

Look back at the readings in Chapters 1, 2, 3, and 6 and complete this chart. (More than one answer may be correct.)

CHAPTER	TITLE	TOPIC	MAIN IDEA
1	Are You Getting Enough Sleep? (pp. 3–4)	_____sleep_____	Going without sleep can be bad for your health.
2	Mika's Homestay in London (pp. 13–14)	_____	You can learn a lot from _____ _____ .
3	The Book of the Future (pp. 23–24)	the e-book	Books in the future will be _____ _____ .
6	Cell Phones: Hang Up or Keep Talking? (pp. 55–56)	_____	_____ _____ _____ .

Compare your answers with a partner.

Using prefixes: <u>un</u>-, <u>im</u>-, <u>in</u>-, <u>ir</u>-

You can change the meaning of many adjectives by adding a prefix that means *not:* un-, im-, in-, ir-.

For example, the word *unimportant* means *not important* and the word *inactive* means *not active.*

Examples:

un-	im-	in-	ir-
uncomfortable	immobile	inconvenient	irregular
unprofitable	impermanent	incomplete	irreplaceable
unwise	impossible	inactive	irresponsible
unimportant	immature	inexperienced	
unhelpful		independent	
unsuccessful			
unhealthy			

A. Add the correct prefix (un-, im-, in-, ir-) to each adjective below to make the meaning negative.

> **Example:** *Is it ____impossible____ to learn a new language in one year?*

1. Do you think sleeping on a cement floor would be very ____comfortable____?

2. Have you ever handed in an ____complete____ homework assignment?

3. Do you think it's ____healthy____ to go without sleep for several days and nights?

4. Would you like to fly with an ____experienced____ pilot?

5. Do you think it's ____wise____ to use a cell phone?

6. Would you like to own an ____profitable____ restaurant?

B. Pair work. Ask a partner the questions from Activity A.

C. Choose six words from the reading that you want to remember. Add them to your vocabulary log on page 172.

Understanding gerunds

A gerund is the *-ing* form of a verb when it is used as a noun. The boldfaced words below are gerunds. In each example, the gerund is the subject of the sentence.

Examples:
Helping others makes you feel good.
Meeting these people was wonderful for each of us.
Developing close relationships is one of the important things in life.
Being involved with Habitat has changed my life.

A. Complete each sentence with a gerund from the box below. (More than one answer is possible.)

developing close relationships	saving money
doing research	sleeping on a cement floor
going without sleep	worrying
starting your own business	using a mobile phone
learning to fly a plane	traveling abroad
making a profit	working in a restaurant
watching television	

1. _____ is really bad for your health.

2. _____ would be difficult.

3. _____ will help you keep in touch with your friends.

4. _____ is an important thing to do.

5. _____ is a wise thing to do.

6. _____ would be a lot of fun.

7. _____ helps relieve stress.

8. _____ is exciting.

B. Pair work. Read the sentences from Activity A to a partner. Find out if your partner agrees or disagrees with each statement.

Example   A: *Going without sleep is really bad for your health.*
   B: *That's true. (or Really? Why is that?)*

Discussion & Writing

A. Which of the following volunteer opportunities would you choose? Why?

1. reading to a blind person

2. cooking for a sick person

3. fixing bicycles for children

4. helping someone learn to read

5. cleaning a house for an older person

B. Being involved with Habitat was an important experience in Mariko Asano's life. Follow the steps below to write about an important experience in your life.

Step 1: Think of some important experiences in your life. List them on a piece of paper.

Example: Important experiences in my life
- *meeting Tina*
- *going to Canada*
- *learning to play the piano*
- *learning to drive a car*
- *spending time with my grandmother*

Step 2: Choose one of the experiences on your list. Collect information about this experience in a chart like the one below.

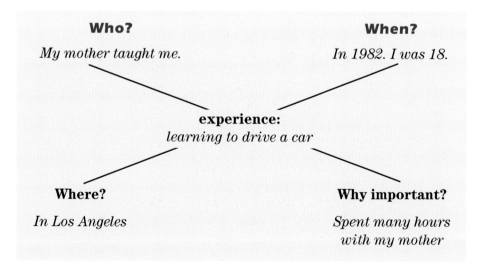

Who?
My mother taught me.

When?
In 1982. I was 18.

experience:
learning to drive a car

Where?
In Los Angeles

Why important?
*Spent many hours
with my mother*

Step 3: Write about your experience. Then tell a partner about the experience.

Example:

Learning to drive a car was an important experience in my life. My mother taught me to drive while my father was away on business . . .

C. Find out about a volunteer organization in your area. Share what you learned with your classmates.

Name of organization: _____

Purpose: _____

_____

Web site: _____

Phone: _____

WORDS TO REMEMBER			
NOUNS	**VERBS**	**ADJECTIVES**	**ADVERBS**
fulfillment	appreciate	(a) close (relationship)	generously
lifestyle	be involved in	valuable	
message	care about	uncomfortable	
organization	volunteer	incomplete	
relationship	grow up	unhealthy	
volunteer	keep (in touch)		
	make (a difference)		
	offer		

Chapter

9 Baseball Fans Around the World

Fan holding an airhorn
in Fukuoka, Japan

Vendor selling refreshments at an American baseball game

*Take me out
to the ballgame,
Take me out
to the crowd,
Buy me some peanuts
and Cracker Jacks,
I don't care if I
never get back.*

—*Jack Norworth,
American songwriter*

Chapter Focus

CONTENT:
The behavior of baseball fans

READING SKILL:
Making predictions

BUILDING VOCABULARY:
Grouping words and phrases

LANGUAGE FOCUS:
Using the verbs *see, hear, watch,* and
feel + object + *-ing* form

Before You Read

A. What do you know about baseball? Study the diagram and read the statements below. Check (√) True or False.

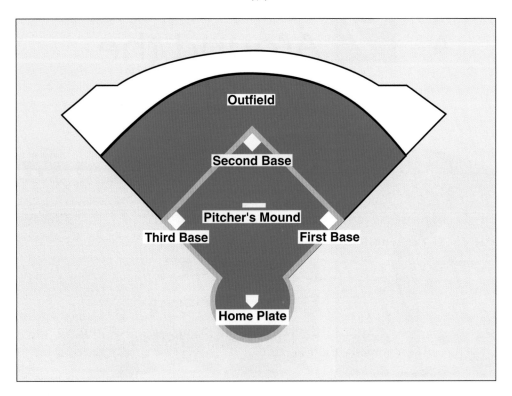

	True	False
1. There are five bases on a baseball field.	☐	☐
2. The baseball pitcher pitches (throws) the ball from first base.	☐	☐
3. The batter bats (hits the ball) from home plate.	☐	☐
4. When a batter hits a home run, he must touch three bases and home plate.	☐	☐

B. Look at the title of the reading on page 87. What do you think the reading will be about?

BASEBALL FANS AROUND THE WORLD

1   Baseball is a very popular sport in Asia, North America, South America, and even Europe. While the rules of baseball are similar from country to country, the behavior of baseball fans is very different. Here's a look at some of the differences in fan behavior
5   around the world.

In Japan

Baseball fans in Japan are loud—really loud. The sound of chants, cheering, drums, and trumpets continues nonstop throughout a baseball game in Japan. When a team goes to bat,[1] their fans sing a different song for each batter at the plate. And even when their team is
10   losing badly, Japanese fans continue to yell and scream. **Foreign baseball players** in Japan are often surprised that the fans never boo[2] a player. According to the American pitcher Brian Warren, baseball is more fun in Japan. "When I used to play in **Venezuela**," Warren said, "fans threw things at me when I didn't pitch well." This
15   never happens in Japan.

When a Japanese player hits a home run, the fans give the biggest cheer of all—a *banzai* cheer. That's when the fans yell with both of their arms above their heads.

In Taiwan

Baseball fans in **Taiwan** are just as loud as the fans in Japan! In
20   Taiwan, many fans use air horns to cheer their team on. These horns are so loud they can really hurt your ears. Taiwanese fans often yell "Charge!" to excite the baseball players. And when a player hits a home run, there is a special tradition. After the player runs around the bases, a young girl presents him with a stuffed animal that looks
25   like his team's mascot.[3]

In the United States

Asian visitors to the United States are often surprised and disappointed by how quiet American baseball fans are. "When I went to a baseball game in San Francisco, everybody was just sitting there watching the game. It was kind of boring," says Barry Lin, a
30   Taiwanese student at the University of California, Berkeley. "Baseball was invented in the United States," Lin says, "but Americans don't seem very excited about their game."

---

[1] **goes to bat**   takes their turn hitting the ball

[2] **boo**   make the noise "boo!" to show disapproval

[3] **mascot**   an animal that is a team's symbol of good luck

It's true. Baseball fans in the United States are some of the quietest in the world. It's common to see baseball fans eating **hot dogs** and **popcorn,** and chatting with friends. "When I go to a baseball game," says Ginger Hanson from San Francisco, "I want to have fun with friends and catch up on[4] their lives. The real reason I go is for the social experience."

In the Dominican Republic

Like the fans in Japan and Taiwan, the fans in the **Dominican Republic** cheer loudly throughout the game. They also sing and dance! Since music and dancing are an important part of Dominican culture, you might even find a *merengue* band moving through the stands at a baseball game.

Despite the music and dancing, many Dominican fans are very serious about baseball. Carol Parmenter, an American living in the Dominican Republic, says, "At Dominican games, you see groups of men drinking small cups of sweet coffee, carefully analyzing every pitch, every hit, every play. American fans don't usually follow the game that closely."

After You Read

Understanding the Text

A. True or False? Read the statements and check (√) True or False.

	True	False
1. This article is primarily about the rules for playing baseball.	☐	☐
2. According to the article, baseball fans are noisy in every country except the Dominican Republic.	☐	☐
3. Venezuelan baseball fans are different from Japanese baseball fans.	☐	☐
4. Japanese fans give a *banzai* cheer when their players get a home run.	☐	☐
5. Air horns are popular among fans in both Taiwan and the United States.	☐	☐
6. Taiwanese baseball fans are a little quieter than Japanese fans.	☐	☐

---

[4] **catch up on** learn new things about

	True	False
7. The word "scream" in line 10 means *to talk quietly*.	☐	☐
8. The word "chatting" in line 35 means *cooking*.	☐	☐
9. You can infer that baseball fans in Japan and Taiwan don't follow the game very closely.	☐	☐
10. You can infer that Brian Warren has played baseball in Japan.	☐	☐

Work with a classmate to correct the false statements.

B. Consider the issues. Work with a partner to answer the questions below.

1. What was the most surprising or interesting thing that you learned in this reading? Why was it surprising or interesting?

2. Do you think it is ever okay to boo someone? Why or why not?

3. Choose a type of sports event you and your partner have attended and answer the questions below.

Sports event: _____

QUESTIONS	ME	MY PARTNER
How often do you cheer?	☐ All the time ☐ Often ☐ Sometimes ☐ Rarely ☐ Never	☐ All the time ☐ Often ☐ Sometimes ☐ Rarely ☐ Never
What do you yell or sing when you cheer?	_____	_____
What percentage of time do you spend standing during a game?	☐ 0–33% ☐ 34–66% ☐ 67–100%	☐ 0–33% ☐ 34–66% ☐ 67–100%
How closely do you watch the game?	☐ Very closely ☐ Somewhat closely ☐ Not very closely	☐ Very closely ☐ Somewhat closely ☐ Not very closely

Which sentence describes you and your partner best at the sports event?

☐ We do the same things.

☐ We do almost the same things.

☐ We do some of the same things.

☐ We don't do the same things.

Reading Skill

Making predictions
When you make a prediction, you guess what will happen. Before you read a story or article, it helps to look it over and predict what it will be about.

Example:
By looking at the title, proper names, and key words on pages 87–88, you can predict the topic of the reading: the behavior of baseball fans in Japan, Taiwan, the United States, and the Dominican Republic.

Look ahead to Chapter 10 (page 96), Chapter 11 (page 107), and Chapter 12 (page 116). Based on the picture and title at the beginning of each chapter, complete each prediction below.

1. I think Chapter 10 is about: ☐ unusual clothing

☐ the history of music

☐ a famous musician

because _____

_____

_____

2. I think Chapter 11 is about: _____

because _____

_____

_____

3. I think Chapter 12 is about: _____

because _____

_____

_____

Compare ideas with your classmates.

Building Vocabulary

Grouping words and phrases

Grouping words and phrases that are similar can help you remember them. For example, grouping the players in different sports will help you remember them.

Baseball players	Soccer players
pitcher	goalie
catcher	forward
first baseman	halfback
outfielder	fullback

A. Group these phrases in the chart below. Some phrases may go in both groups.

chat with friends	have fun with friends	yell and scream
cheer	hit home runs	use air horns
eat during the game	run around the bases	watch the game
go to bat	sing and dance	

THINGS THAT BASEBALL PLAYERS DO	THINGS THAT BASEBALL FANS DO
_____	_____
_____	_____
_____	_____
_____	_____
_____	_____
_____	_____

B. Add three words or phrases to each group below. (You can look back at the readings in Chapters 1, 2, 4 and 5 for ideas.)

THINGS PEOPLE DO WHEN THEY GO WITHOUT SLEEPING	THINGS PEOPLE DO WHEN THEY ARE LEARNING A FOREIGN LANGUAGE	THINGS RESTAURANT OWNERS DO
hallucinate	mispronounce words	clean the restaurant up
lose weight		make money

C. Choose six words from the reading that you want to remember. Add them to your vocabulary log on page 173.

Language Focus

> **Using the verbs <u>see</u>, <u>hear</u>, <u>watch</u>, and <u>feel</u> + object + <u>-ing</u> form**
>
> **Form:**
>
> see
> hear $\Big|$ + object + *-ing* form of verb
> watch
> feel
>
> **Examples:**
>
> - It's common to **see people eating** hot dogs.
> - At Dominican games, you **see men drinking coffee** and **analyzing** every pitch.
>
> **Meaning**
> We use the verbs *see, hear, watch,* and *feel* with an *-ing* form to show that the activity or action is continuous or ongoing.

A. Complete the following sentences with a verb + **ing**. (More than one answer may be correct.)

1. It's common to see Americans _____ popcorn and talking to friends at a baseball game.

2. In the Dominican Republic, you can see fans _____ and dancing at baseball games.

3. When I went to a game in Japan, I saw many fans _____ very loudly.

4. It's fun to watch my favorite player _____ home runs.

5. At the beach, you can see people _____ in the ocean.

6. I heard you _____ very loudly last night. Please be quieter tonight.

B. What do you see in the illustration below? Identify five things.

> **Example:** *I see people cheering.*
> *I see someone . . .*
> *I see a player . . .*

C. Complete the sentences below with information about a sport in your country.

Sport: _____

1. It's common to see fans _____

2. It's not common to see fans _____

3. At games here, you often see _____

4. At games here, you don't usually see _____

Discussion & Writing

A. Choose one of the sports events below and complete the chart.

basketball game   soccer game   golf match
tennis match   table tennis game   volleyball game

SPORTS EVENT: _____	
THINGS YOU SEE	**THINGS YOU HEAR**
players kicking the ball	fans yelling

Read the information in your chart aloud, but don't identify the sport. See if your classmates can name it.

Example:

A: At this sports event you see players running and jumping.
B: Is it basketball?

B. Pair work. Interview a classmate about his or her favorite sport to watch. Record the answers in the chart below.

1. What's your favorite sport to watch? _____

2. When did you first watch this sport? _____

3. How often do you watch this sport? _____

4. What do you like about this sport? _____

Tell your classmates about your partner's favorite sport to watch.

Example:

My partner's favorite sport to watch is ice hockey. She first watched this sport when she was 12 years old. Now she often watches games on television, and she usually goes to about three games a year. She likes this sport because it's very fast.

WORDS TO REMEMBER		
NOUNS	**VERBS**	**ADJECTIVES**
behavior	catch up on	boring
fan	chat with	common
rules	cheer	loud
tradition	scream	
	yell	

Chapter ▲ 10 Vanessa-Mae: A 21st Century Musician

Vanessa-Mae

I've always felt that good music, if it is well played, will touch anyone anywhere.

—Vanessa-Mae,
*Singaporean musician
(1977–)*

Chapter Focus

CONTENT:
A young musician's life

READING SKILL:
Dealing with unfamiliar words

BUILDING VOCABULARY:
Understanding suffixes

LANGUAGE FOCUS:
Showing a contrast with *although*

Before You Read

A. Who is your favorite musician? What is your favorite song or piece of music by this person? Share your answers with a partner.

Example:

A: *I really like . . .*
B: *What's (her/his) best song?*
A: *I think it's . . .*

B. Scan the reading on pages 97–98 and complete the Previewing Chart below.

PREVIEWING CHART

Title of the article: _____

Names of people and places in the article (List three more.)	Key words (What words appear several times? List three more.)
Singapore	piano
_____	_____
_____	_____
_____	_____

Based on your chart, what do you think the article is about?

Reading Passage

VANESSA-MAE: A 21ST Century Musician

1   Vanessa-Mae was born in **Singapore** in 1977. Her mother was Chinese, and her father was from **Thailand.** At the age of four, Vanessa-Mae moved to London, England with her mother and stepfather.

     As a young child, Vanessa-Mae was already a talented[1] musician. She
5   took her first piano lesson when she was three years old and her first violin lesson when she was five.

Developing Skills

     Vanessa-Mae studied music at the **Central Conservatory of China** in Beijing. She was the youngest student the Conservatory had ever

---

[1] **talented**   very good; with great ability

accepted. She also took lessons at the famous **Royal College of Music**
in London. The director of the college described Vanessa-Mae as "a true
child prodigy[2] — like **Mozart** and **Mendelssohn.**"

When Vanessa-Mae was just eight years old, she had to make a big
decision. She was equally gifted[3] at both the violin and the piano,
but she had to concentrate on just one instrument. Although she
had just won a prize at a famous piano competition, Vanessa-Mae
chose the violin.

At the age of nine, Vanessa-Mae went to **Germany** to take violin
classes for advanced students. The best students were usually
chosen to be a part of the recitals[4] just once or twice. Vanessa-Mae
was chosen four times. These were her first performances in front of
an audience.

By the time she was ten years old, Vanessa-Mae had studied the
violin at some of the best schools in the world. She made her first
professional appearance in 1987 with the Philharmonic Orchestra
in London.

Vanessa-Mae often played Mozart concertos. A concerto is a piece
of music written for one or more solo instruments accompanied by[5]
an orchestra.

Accomplishments

By the time she was twelve, Vanessa-Mae had played with
orchestras all over the world as a soloist. She had also released[6] three
classical recordings.

Although she loved classical music, Vanessa-Mae wanted to
experiment with other kinds of music. At fourteen, she began to
combine the traditional sound of her acoustic[7] violin with the sounds
made from her new electric violin. She called this music "techno-
acoustic fusion." Vanessa-Mae loved the music that the two types of
violins made together. Her first album with techno-acoustic fusion
music was called *The Violin Player.* It was an instant success and
sold in over twenty countries. It was even a hit on the best-selling
music charts.

No longer just a classical musician, Vanessa-Mae was asked to
perform at international rock concerts. At a concert in Switzerland,

---

[2] **prodigy**   genius; person with great ability

[3] **gifted**   talented

[4] **recitals**   performances by music or dance students

[5] **accompanied by**   along with; together with

[6] **released**   made available for sale

[7] **acoustic**   a musical instrument that is not electronic

the audience of 50,000 people gave her a twenty-minute ovation.[8] The crowd did not want her to stop playing.

45   Vanessa-Mae has sometimes been criticized for not just playing classical music. However, she feels it is important to introduce violin music to a new audience. "If, as a result [of my music], people see the violin as a fresh, up-to-date[9] instrument, that's fine with me."

After You Read

Understanding the Text

A. Sequence of events. Number these events in Vanessa-Mae's life from first (1) to last (7).

_____ She moved from Singapore to London with her mother and stepfather.

_____ She went to Germany to take advanced violin classes.

_____ She made her first professional appearance.

__1__ She was born in Singapore.

_____ She decided to concentrate on the violin instead of the piano.

_____ She studied music in China.

_____ She started playing "techno-acoustic fusion" music.

B. Inferencing. What can you infer from the statements below? Circle the best answer.

1. Vanessa-Mae studied music at the Central Conservatory of China in Beijing. She was the youngest student the Conservatory had ever accepted. You can infer from this that _____.

   a. the Conservatory only accepts young students.

   b. the Conservatory was the only school that accepted Vanessa-Mae.

   c. Vanessa-Mae was very talented when she was young.

2. At a concert in Switzerland, 50,000 people gave Vanessa-Mae a twenty-minute ovation. You can infer from this that _____.

   a. The audience loved her music.

   b. The audience didn't like her music.

   c. Her music was very unusual.

---

[8] **ovation**   cheering by the audience

[9] **up-to-date**   contemporary; modern

3. By the time she was twelve, Vanessa-Mae had played with orchestras all over the world. You can infer from this that _____.

    a. Vanessa-Mae traveled a lot before she was twelve.

    b. Vanessa-Mae could speak many different languages when she was young.

    c. Vanessa-Mae never played solo before she was twelve.

C. Consider the issues. Work with a partner to answer the questions below.

1. How would you describe Vanessa-Mae? Make five sentences using words from columns A and B.

> **Example:** *I think Vanessa-Mae is successful because she works very hard.*

	A		B
I think Vanessa-Mae is	interesting unusual creative talented successful smart _____ _____	because	she experiments with different kinds of music. she has lived in many countries. she has made several recordings. she started playing music when she was very young. she works very hard. she was equally gifted at the piano and violin. she is beautiful. _____ _____

2. If you could interview Vanessa-Mae, what questions would you ask her? Write your ideas.

> **Examples:** *Do you feel nervous when you perform in front of an audience?*
> *How long did you study in China?*

    a. Do you _____?

    b. Did you _____?

    c. Who _____?

    d. What _____?

    e. When _____?

    f. Where _____?

g. Why _____?

h. How _____?

Reading Skill

Dealing with unfamiliar words

When you are reading a paragraph in English, many of the words may be unfamiliar. However, stopping to look up every word in a dictionary can make it more difficult to understand the paragraph. Instead, try to get the general meaning of the paragraph from the words you already know. Then use context to guess the meaning of other important words.

A. Answer these questions with information from the paragraphs below. **Do not write the missing words in the paragraph.**

1. Where was Midori born?

2. What instrument did her mother play?

3. Where did Midori's mother take her when she was a baby?

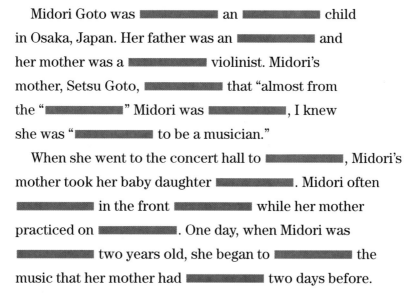

    Midori Goto was ▆▆▆▆▆▆ an ▆▆▆▆▆▆▆ child in Osaka, Japan. Her father was an ▆▆▆▆▆▆ and her mother was a ▆▆▆▆▆▆ violinist. Midori's mother, Setsu Goto, ▆▆▆▆▆▆ that "almost from the "▆▆▆▆▆▆" Midori was ▆▆▆▆▆▆, I knew she was "▆▆▆▆▆▆ to be a musician."

    When she went to the concert hall to ▆▆▆▆▆▆, Midori's mother took her baby daughter ▆▆▆▆▆▆. Midori often ▆▆▆▆▆▆ in the front ▆▆▆▆▆▆ while her mother practiced on ▆▆▆▆▆▆. One day, when Midori was ▆▆▆▆▆▆ two years old, she began to ▆▆▆▆▆▆ the music that her mother had ▆▆▆▆▆▆ two days before.

B. Do you need to understand every word in a reading? Why or why not?

Understanding suffixes

Suffixes come at the end of words. They help you know if a word is a noun, verb, or adjective. For example, many adjectives end with these suffixes:

Suffix	Sample adjectives	Meaning
-able	portable	can be carried
	profitable	can make a profit
-ous	famous	having fame
	cautious	having caution
-ful	helpful	full of help
	harmful	full of harm
-less	heartless	without heart
	friendless	without friends

A. Underline the suffix in each word. Then tell what you think each word means.

1. count<u>able</u>   *can be counted*

2. washable _____

3. readable _____

4. dangerous _____

5. spacious _____

6. fearful _____

7. sorrowful _____

8. loveless _____

8. fearless _____

10. hopeless _____

B. Choose six words from the reading that you want to remember. Add them to your vocabulary log on page 173.

Showing a contrast with <u>although</u>
The words *although* and *even though* show a contrast between two ideas in a sentence or an unexpected result.

Example	Meaning
• Although Vanessa-Mae won a prize at a piano competition, she chose to study the violin. ⟶	She won a prize at a piano competition; however, she chose to continue studying the violin.
• She experiments with different kinds of music although she loves classical music. ⟶	She loves classical music; however, she experiments with different kinds of music.
• She was in a violin class for advanced students even though she was only nine years old. ⟶	She was only nine years old; however, she was in a violin class for advanced students.

A. Circle the word in parentheses that best completes each sentence.

1. Although he selected a book that looked easy, he (could/couldn't) read it.

2. He (is/isn't) losing weight even though he eats a lot every day.

3. Although I selected a school with few Japanese students, there (were/weren't) two in each class.

4. Although she went without sleep for 24 hours, she (was/wasn't) able to think clearly.

5. He (could/couldn't) get a job in the airplane industry although he knew how to fly a plane.

6. Although she usually looks forward to playing the piano, she (wants/doesn't want) to practice today.

7. Millions of people (are/aren't) using cell phones even though they might be harmful.

B. Complete these sentences with your own ideas.

1. Although she felt tired, _____

_____

2. Although he took piano lessons for many years, _____

_____

3. Although we know that smoking is harmful, _____

_____

4. Although he mispronounced many words, _____

_____

5. He went outside even though _____

_____

6. She felt tired even though _____

_____

7. Susan did poorly on the test even though _____

_____

8. Even though Linda studied French for five years, _____

_____

9. Although I like to eat fish, _____

_____

10. Although he's only eight years old, _____

_____

Discussion & Writing

A. Follow the instructions below to write a timeline for one of your classmates.

Step 1: List five or more important events in your life.

Example: *cut my foot and went to the hospital*
my brother was born
started school
started ballet lessons

Step 2: Exchange lists with a classmate. Ask questions to find out when each event happened.

Example: *A: When did you cut your foot?*
B: When I was three.
A: What year was that?
B: 1988.

Step 3: Use your classmate's answers to make a timeline about his or her life.

Example:

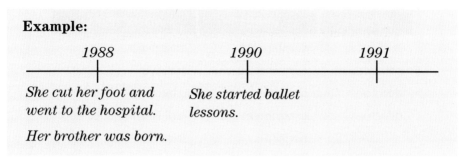

1988   1990   1991

She cut her foot and   She started ballet
went to the hospital.   lessons.

Her brother was born.

B. Collect 6 to 8 facts about someone famous. Use the information to make a biographical timeline of this person.

C. Find someone who answers <u>yes</u> to the first question in Box 1 and 2 below. Then ask the follow-up questions to get more details.

Example: A: *Do you play a musical instrument?*
B: *Yes, I do.*
A: *What instrument do you play?*
B: *I play the guitar.*

1	2
A: Do you play a musical instrument?	A: Have you ever been to a concert?
B: _____	B: _____
A: What instrument do you play?	A: Where was the concert?
B: _____	B: _____
A: What kind of music do you like to play?	A: What kind of music was it?
B: _____	B: _____
A: Have you ever performed in front of an audience?	A: Was it a good concert?
B: _____	B: _____

Share what you learned with your classmates.

Example: *Mei plays the piano. She likes to play jazz.*

WORDS TO REMEMBER		
NOUNS	**VERBS**	**ADJECTIVES**
audience	combine	advanced
competition	concentrate on	creative
decision	describe	gifted
director	experiment with	(an) instant (success)
	perform	talented
	win (a prize)	

Chapter

11 How Safe Is Nuclear Power?

Nuclear power provides 16% of the world's electricity. There are more than 400 nuclear power plants in operation in the world today.

It's better to be safe than sorry.

—*American saying*

Chapter Focus

CONTENT:
Nuclear power

READING SKILL:
Writing margin notes

BUILDING VOCABULARY:
Learning word forms

LANGUAGE FOCUS:
Using a verb + *that* clause

Before You Read

A. What forms of energy are used where you live? Check (√) your answers.

☐ coal   ☐ solar (sun) power
☐ oil   ☐ wind power
☐ nuclear power   ☐ _____

B. Scan the reading on pages 108–109 and complete the "Previewing Chart" below.

PREVIEWING CHART

Title of the article: _____

Names of places in the article (List three more.)	Key words (What words appear several times? List three more.)
Japan	radiation
_____	_____
_____	_____
_____	_____

Based on your chart, what do you think the article is about?

Reading Passage

HOW SAFE IS NUCLEAR POWER?

1   On September 30, 1999, there was an accident at a nuclear plant in Tokaimura, Japan. On that day, three plant employees accidentally poured too much uranium into a tank,[1] which led to a leak of radiation.[2] At least 90 people were exposed to[3] high radiation. One
5   worker died.

Other countries have had similar accidents. There was a close call[4] at a nuclear plant at **Three Mile Island** in the United States. On March 28, 1979, there was a reactor meltdown at this plant. A reactor

---

[1] **tank**   large metal container

[2] **leak of radiation**   dangerous nuclear material going into the air

[3] **were exposed to**   had contact with

[4] **a close call**   a dangerous situation that could have been worse

meltdown happens when the fuel inside a reactor melts.[5] Unless immediate safety measures[6] are taken, a meltdown can lead to radiation leaking into the atmosphere.[7]

Probably the most famous nuclear accident occurred at a plant in Chernobyl, in the **former Soviet Union.** The accident happened on April 26, 1986, when things went terribly wrong[8] during an experiment. This caused a meltdown so serious that the top of a reactor exploded into the sky. Radiation leaked into the atmosphere for more than a week. Wind carried some of the radioactive pollution over large parts of Europe. Many deaths and birth defects throughout Europe have resulted from this horrible event.

Reactor core and cooling pool in a nuclear power plant

The idea of using nuclear power as a form of energy grew out of weapons research[9] before and during **World War II** (1939–1945). Nuclear power was first used to make electricity on December 20, 1951. By the 1960s, nuclear energy was becoming cheap to produce, and utility companies[10] were building plenty of plants. However, in the 1970s, there were concerns about the possibilities of nuclear disasters and environmental problems. Then, those concerns came true[11] with the tragedy at Chernobyl and the near-disaster at Three Mile Island.

Today, supporters of nuclear energy say it is a necessary source of power. This is especially true in countries like Japan, which depends on nuclear energy for about 35% of its power. Obviously, taking away that source of energy could badly hurt the economy. Also, while minor accidents sometimes happen at nuclear plants, most are contained without deaths or serious injuries.

For now, nuclear energy is probably not going away. Citizens should demand that government agencies have very strict safety measures for nuclear power plants. At the same time, we must find other safer and cheaper sources of energy.

---

[5] **melts**   changes from a solid to a liquid

[6] **safety measures**   actions to make something safe

[7] **atmosphere**   air around our earth

[8] **things went terribly wrong**   very bad things happened

[9] **weapons research**   work to develop military equipment for war

[10] **utility companies**   companies that provide gas, electricity, or water

[11] **come true**   happen; become real

After You Read

Understanding the Text

A. True or False? Read the sentences and check (√) True or False.

	True	False
1. The main idea of this reading is that nuclear energy is a safe source of power.	☐	☐
2. The accident at a nuclear plant in Tokaimura, Japan occurred because workers forgot to put uranium into a tank.	☐	☐
3. A reactor meltdown occurs when the fuel inside a nuclear reactor melts.	☐	☐
4. A meltdown is dangerous because radiation can leak into the atmosphere.	☐	☐
5. As a result of the accident at Chernobyl, people in the area were exposed to small amounts of radiation.	☐	☐
6. The pronoun *it* in line 34 refers to *today*.	☐	☐
7. The words *taking away* in line 36 mean *removing*.	☐	☐
8. You can infer from lines 25–28 that nuclear power was not used to generate electricity in the 1940s.	☐	☐

Work with your classmates to correct the false statements.

B. What happened at the places below? Look for information on pages 108–109 to complete the chart.

DATE	PLACE	WHAT HAPPENED?
March 28, 1979	**Three Mile Island** Country: _____U.S._____	a nuclear reactor _____
_____	**Chernobyl** Country: _____	a nuclear accident; the top of a nuclear reactor _____
_____	**Tokaimura** Country: _____	a radiation _____

Compare charts with your classmates.

C. Consider the issues. Work with a partner to answer the questions below.

1. What are the advantages and disadvantages of using nuclear power? Make a chart like this on a piece of paper. Add these ideas to it.

- ~~it produces cheap electricity~~
- radiation might leak into the atmosphere
- people might be exposed to radiation
- radioactive pollution can cause birth defects
- serious nuclear accidents are rare

ADVANTAGES	DISADVANTAGES
It produces cheap electricity	

Compare ideas with a classmate.

A: One advantage of using nuclear power is that . . .
B: I agree. But one disadvantage is that . . .

2. What is your opinion? Check (✓) "I think" or "I don't think." Then finish the sentence with a reason.

Example:

I think	I don't think	
✓	☐	nuclear power is dangerous

because *radiation might leak into the atmosphere.*

I think	I don't think	
a. ☐	☐	nuclear power is dangerous

because _____.

I think	I don't think	
b. ☐	☐	we should stop using nuclear

power because _____.

I think	I don't think	
c. ☐	☐	nuclear power will be more popular

in the future because _____.

Compare your ideas with a partner.

Writing margin notes

As you read, try writing your thoughts and reactions in the margin. Your margin notes might be questions, phrases, single words, or symbols. Writing margin notes can help you read more carefully and actively.

Example:

*	For now, nuclear energy is probably not going away. Citizens should demand that government agencies have very strict safety measures for nuclear power plants. At the same time, we must find other safer and cheaper sources of energy.

How do we do this?

Agree.

Write margin notes as you read the paragraph below. Use two of the phrases or symbols in the box below.

Sample margin notes

Phrases	Symbols
Interesting.	!
Very interesting.	!!
I don't understand.	?
Important.	*
I agree.	√
I disagree.	×

We all breathe the air that surrounds earth. The air is made up mainly of gases: around 78% nitrogen, 21% oxygen, and 1% carbon dioxide, other gases, and water vapor. Human beings breathe more than six quarts (5.7 liters) of air every minute. Because air is so basic to life, it is very important to keep the air clean by reducing or preventing air pollution.

—*The World Almanac*

Compare your notes with a partner.

Building Vocabulary

Learning word forms

When you learn a new word, it's useful to learn other forms of the same word. You can find these forms in a dictionary. For example, if you know the verb *react*, you can use a dictionary to find the noun forms *reaction* and *reactor*.

A. Complete the chart below by adding the missing noun form(s). Then check your ideas by looking in a dictionary.

	Nouns	Verbs
1.	*reaction, reactor*	react
2.		radiate
3.		pollute
4.		result
5.		research
6.		electrify
7.		contain
8.		support
9.		injure
10.		inspect

B. Complete each question with a noun from Activity A. Then ask a partner your questions.

1. Are you a s_____ of nuclear power?

2. Why is air p_____ a problem in the world today?

3. Is nuclear r_____ dangerous?

4. What do you use e_____ for?

5. Have you ever had a serious i_____?

6. What was one r_____ of the nuclear meltdown at Chernobyl?

C. Choose six words from the reading that you want to remember. Add them to your vocabulary log on page 174.

Using a verb + <u>that</u> clause

We often use the verbs below to state an idea or opinion. It is common to use a *that* clause after these verbs.

admit	believe	explain	know	think
agree	claim	feel	reply	
argue	estimate	insist	say	

Examples:

I agree that we need stricter safety measures for nuclear power plants.

I think that nuclear plants need to have stricter safety measures.

You can remove the word *that* after all of the verbs above except *argue, explain,* or *reply.*

Examples:

I thought that he was right. **OR** I thought he was right.

BUT

He argued that he was right. **OR** She explained that she was Jon's mother.

A. The word **that** was removed from each of these sentences. Put the word **that** in the appropriate place in each sentence.

that

Example: *Even though people know ∧ they use too much electricity, they refuse to be more careful.*

1. Some people say we should close down all nuclear power plants.

2. How many of you agree we need to stop using so much electricity?

3. Many people think we need to build more nuclear power plants.

4. I feel we should spend more money on new technologies that can provide cheap and safe electricity.

5. He said he didn't have an opinion about nuclear power.

B. Complete each sentence with your own idea.

1. I think that nuclear power _____

2. The article in this chapter said that _____

3. Supporters of nuclear power agree that _____

4. I believe that in the future _____

Read each sentence to your partner. Then, read each sentence again without **that**.

A: Pair work. How could we reduce the amount of pollution in the world? Add your suggestions to the chart below.

Suggestions for reducing pollution

- use solar-powered cars
- limit the number of cars per family
- close factories that pollute the air
- _____
- _____
- _____

Share suggestions with your classmates and then complete the sentence below.

I think the best suggestion is to _____

B. What are the most serious problems in the world today? Add two ideas to the list below.

terrible diseases like _____.
starvation
terrorism
air pollution

_____

_____

For each item on your list, think of something people can do to help solve this problem.

Example: *To help end starvation in the world, people can send money to poor countries.*

WORDS TO REMEMBER			
NOUNS	**VERBS**	**ADJECTIVES**	**ADVERBS**
accident	come true	environmental	accidentally
atmosphere	depend on	horrible	terribly
energy	explode	necessary	
injury	go wrong		
pollution	melt		
safety measures	react		
reaction	result from		
source	take away		

Chapter

12 Love at First Sight

"*Love at first sight—*
I can't explain it,
but it's real and
happens all the time."

—*Taylor Stanley,*
American actress (1976–)

Chapter Focus

CONTENT:
Falling in love

READING SKILL:
Asking yourself questions while you read

BUILDING VOCABULARY:
Using a learner's dictionary

LANGUAGE FOCUS:
Using the past continuous

Before You Read

A. Look at the two people on page 116. What is their relationship? Check a box and compare answers with a classmate.

☐ good friends ☐ two people who just met

☐ brother and sister ☐ classmates

☐ boyfriend and girlfriend ☐ husband and wife

B. Scan the reading on pages 117–119 and complete the chart.

PREVIEWING CHART	
Title of the article: _____	
Names of people and places in the article (List three more.)	**Key words** (What words appear several times? List three more.)
Anne	love
_____	_____
_____	_____
_____	_____

Based on your chart, what do you think the article is about?

Reading Passage

LOVE AT FIRST SIGHT

1   *It was love at first sight.* It's always exciting to hear those words. But do people *really* believe in love at first sight? We asked 40 Americans this question—18 men and 22 women. Thirteen people (32%) said they believed in love at first sight; 27 people (68%) said they didn't.

5   Next, we wanted to find out who believed in love at first sight and who didn't. We were surprised to find that both younger and older people believed they could fall in love in a few short seconds. We also learned that people from many different professions had love-at-first-sight experiences. These people included a scientist, an artist, a
10 dancer, and a computer programmer.

    What was the most interesting thing we learned in our study? More men believed in love at first sight than women: 44% of the men believed in this kind of love, while only 27% of the women did. Here's what some of the men and women in our survey said about love at first sight.

Name: John
Occupation: Artist
Age: 30

15 "Yes, I believe in love at first sight. It happened to me. I was at a party several years ago when I saw Luisa. I knew she was the one for me when her eyes flashed back at me.[1] It was like they looked into my
20 heart, read my life story, and said, 'I like what I see, and want to be with you.' That night at the party, I went over to Luisa and asked her to dance. She said, 'Of course, I was waiting for you to ask.' That was three
25 years ago, and we're still together."

Name: Mark
Occupation: Salesman
Age: 35

"I didn't use to believe in love at first sight, but now I do. About four years ago, I was giving a sales presentation when this amazing[2] woman walked into the room.
30 We made eye contact[3] and my heart started beating faster.[4] After my presentation, I introduced myself, and she and I went out for dinner the next night. We talked and talked, and by the end of
35 the evening, I was truly in love with her. That feeling of love at first sight was like nothing else. In just a few seconds, I was filled with intense[5] energy and passion. Anne and I got married a year later."

---

[1] **her eyes flashed back at me** she looked into my eyes with a lot of emotion

[2] **amazing** fantastic

[3] **made eye contact** looked into each other's eyes

[4] **heart started beating faster** heart began to move very quickly

[5] **intense** very strong

Name: Emily
Occupation: College student
Age: 23

40 "No, I don't believe in love at first sight. Love comes later in a relationship. When I met my boyfriend, I felt something tingly.[6] I guess you could call it puppy love,[7] but it wasn't true love. It took
45 about a year for true love to develop between us."

Name: Carol
Occupation: Writer
Age: 37

"Do I believe in love at first sight? No, not really. Love is based on trust and shared experiences and values.[8] Love
50 takes time to develop. You fall in love slowly by talking to a special person, writing him love letters, fighting, making up.[9] The key to love is staying excited about the other person, month
55 after month, year after year."

Name: Sarah
Occupation: High school senior
Age: 18

"I don't think love at first sight happens very often, but of course it happens sometimes. It makes me happy to think that it might happen to me. If I didn't
60 believe love at first sight was possible, it would be really depressing."

---

[6] **felt something tingly**   had feelings of excitement

[7] **puppy love**   early feelings of love that are not serious

[8] **shared experiences and values**   things that two people do together and ideas they agree on

[9] **making up**   apologizing to each other after an argument

The authors sent an e-mail message to 75 Americans, asking them to answer some questions about love at first sight. Forty people responded. The youngest person who answered the questions was 15, and the oldest person was 62. Many of the people who responded were students; others were teachers, lawyers, and other professionals.

After You Read

Understanding the Text

A. Multiple choice. For each item below, circle the best answer.

1. This reading is primarily about _____.

   a. the difference between love and friendship

   b. falling in love at first sight

   c. how true love develops

2. The following statement is true about the people in the study:

   a. 32% of the men and women don't believe in love at first sight.

   b. 56% of the men believe in love at first sight.

   c. 27% of the women believe in love at first sight.

3. We know for certain that John and Luisa _____.

   a. are married

   b. met three years ago

   c. are going to get married

4. The following people believe in love at first sight _____.

   a. John, Mark, and Sarah

   b. Mark, Emily, and Sarah

   c. John, Mark, and Carol

5. You can infer that:

    a. Emily has had a love-at-first-sight experience.

    b. Anne is in love with Mark.

    c. John, Emily, and Carol are very good friends.

6. In line 60 of the reading passage, the word *depressing* means:

    a. impressive

    b. exciting

    c. sad

7. The author's purpose in writing this article was to _____.

    a. show that only young people believe in love at first sight

    b. report on an informal study about love at first sight

    c. report on a serious, scientific study about love at first sight

NAME, PROFESSION, AGE	BELIEVES IN LOVE AT FIRST SIGHT?	REASON
John, artist, 30	Yes	It happened to him.
Mark, ,		
Emily, ,		
Carol, ,		
Sarah, ,		

B. Consider the issues. Work with a partner to answer the questions below.

    1. In the reading, five people give their opinions about love at first sight. Look at the reading and complete this chart.

    2. What can you conclude from the information in the chart above? Check (√) one or more of the boxes below.

        ☐ Both of the men believe in love at first sight.

        ☐ All of the women believe in love at first sight.

        ☐ The three people in their 30's believe in love at first sight.

        ☐ The people who have experienced love at first sight believe it's real.

3. Which statement describes your reaction to the reading. Check
(√) one or more statements or write your own.

☐ I think this study was interesting.

☐ This study was not scientific, so it was not interesting to me.

☐ I was surprised that more men believed in love at first sight
than women.

☐ I would like to see a similar study of 40 people from my
country.

☐ _____ .

Reading Skill

Asking yourself questions while you read
As you read, it helps to stop and ask yourself questions to check
your comprehension. Here are some questions you can ask
yourself while you are reading:

- Do I understand this?
- Do I know what this word means?
- What information do I remember?
- Do I need to read this again?

A. Reread the **first paragraph** of the article on page 117 and then
ask and answer these questions:

QUESTIONS	ANSWERS
1. Do I understand the information in this paragraph?	_____
2. Do I know what the phrase "love at first sight" means?	_____
3. Do I need to read this again?	_____

B. Reread the **second paragraph** on page 117 and ask and answer
these questions:

QUESTIONS	ANSWERS
1. Do I understand the information in this paragraph?	_____
2. Do I know what a "love-at-first-sight experience" is?	_____
3. What information do I remember from this paragraph?	_____

C. Now reread the **third paragraph** on page 117–118. Ask yourself three questions of your own. Share your questions with a partner.

QUESTIONS	ANSWERS
1. _____	_____
2. _____	_____
3. _____	_____

Building Vocabulary

Using a learner's dictionary
You can get a lot of useful information from a dictionary for English language learners. Here are some things you can find:

- sample sentences to help you understand new words

- information to help you pronounce words

- the meaning of idioms

A. Read these statements and check (√) True or False. Then use the dictionary entry below and on page 124 to check your answers.

	True	False
1. The word *love* can be a noun or a verb.	☐	☐
2. The opposite of *love* is *hate*.	☐	☐
3. In tennis, the word *love* means *one*.	☐	☐
4. The phrase *to fall in love* is an idiom.	☐	☐

love *noun* **1** a very strong feeling of affection for somebody/something: a. *It was love at first sight.* b. *I don't think she's marrying him for love!* c. *his love for his country* ◊ The opposite is **hate** or **hatred**. **2** [sing] a strong feeling of interest in or enjoyment of something: *a love of adventure* **3** a thing in which you are very interested: *Computers are the love of his life these days.* **4** a person who is loved: *Of course, my love.* **5** (used in tennis) a score of zero: *"15-love,"* called the umpire. **6** (informal) a way of ending a letter to a friend or a member of your family: *Lots of love from us all, Denise.*

IDIOM **be in love (with somebody)** to have a strong feeling of affection and attraction (for somebody): *They're very much in love (with each other).*

IDIOM **fall in love (with somebody)** to start to feel a strong affection and attraction for somebody: *They fell in love and were married within two months.*

love *verb* **1** to have a strong feeling of affection for somebody/something: a. *"Do you love him?" "Yes, very much."* b. *It's wonderful to be loved.* **2** to love very much or to enjoy: a. *I love summertime! My father loves to listen to music.* c. *"Would you like to come?" "I'd love to." The cat just loves it when you pet her right here.*

B. Identify the word **love** in each sentence below as a noun or verb. Then write the number of the dictionary definition from Activity A.

	Noun	Verb	Definition #
1. I'd love to see you again sometime.	☐	☑	2
2. Come live with me and be my love.	☐	☐	
3. I love you more than I can say.	☐	☐	
4. I've lost my love for car racing.	☐	☐	
5. Blond is the color of my true love's hair.	☐	☐	
6. The score is 30-love.	☐	☐	

C. Choose six words from the reading that you want to remember. Add them to your vocabulary log on page 174.

Language Focus

Using the past continuous
Form: *was/were* + **present participle**
Meaning: The past continuous shows that an activity was ongoing or continued over a period of time in the past.

Example:

- She said, "I **was waiting** for you to ask."

- I **was giving** a presentation when this amazing woman walked in the room.

A. Circle the simple past or past continuous verb in parentheses that best completes each sentence.

1. I was at a party several years ago when I (met / was meeting) Luisa.

2. My wife and I met when we (studied / were studying) at Boston University.

3. The chair (broke / was breaking) when I sat down on it.

4. The police stopped him because he (drove / was driving) very fast.

5. No one (called / was calling) while you were out of the office.

6. She (traveled / was traveling) to the Philippines three times last year.

Discussion & Writing

A. Group work. What do you think these quotes mean? For each quote, write a short explanation in the chart below. Then compare ideas with the other groups in your class.

Quote	Explanation
Love is a great beautifier. *Louisa May Alcott (1832–1888), American writer*	*Love makes a person more beautiful. When you are in love you are happy. When you are happy, you look better.*
Love makes the world go round. *French Proverb*	
Love is blind. *William Shakespeare (1564–1616), English playwright and poet*	
Love conquers[11] all things. *Virgil (70–19 B.C.), Roman poet*	

B. Group work. In a group of four to six people, discuss one of the questions below.

- Do you think it's possible to fall in love at first sight?
- Do you think love makes a person more beautiful?
- Do you think love makes the world go round?
- Do you think love conquers all things?

---

[11] **conquers** wins over

Now follow the steps below.

Step 1.   Ask each person in your group to answer the question you chose and record their answers below. Then add your own answer.

Question: _____

Classmates' Names	Yes	No
_____	____	____
_____	____	____
_____	____	____
_____	____	____
_____	____	____
_____	____	____

Step 2.   Count the number of people who answered <u>yes</u>. Then report your group's answers to the class.

Example: *Four people believe in love at first sight.*
Two people don't believe in love at first sight.

Step 3.   Listen to the other groups' reports. Do your classmates' answers surprise you? Why or why not?

WORDS TO REMEMBER		
NOUNS	**VERBS**	**ADJECTIVES**
eye contact	be based on	amazing
profession	fall (in love)	depressing
(love at first) sight	get married	intense
survey	include	
	make up	

Chapter ▲ **13** A Day in the Life of a Freshman

A group blind date in Seoul, Korea

All work and no play makes Jack a dull[1] boy.

—American saying

▼ Chapter Focus

CONTENT:
A university student's life

READING SKILL:
Using context clues

BUILDING VOCABULARY:
Understanding two-word verbs

LANGUAGE FOCUS:
Expressing cause and effect with
so + noun/adjective + *that*

---

[1] **dull**   not interesting; boring

Before You Read

A. How likely is it[2] for a university freshman to do each activity below? Check (√) your answers. Compare ideas with a classmate.

ON A TYPICAL DAY, IT'S . . .				
VERY LIKELY	LIKELY	UNLIKELY	VERY UNLIKELY	FOR A UNIVERSITY FRESHMAN TO _____ .
☐	☐	☐	☐	a. get up early
☐	☐	☐	☐	b. skip a class
☐	☐	☐	☐	c. always do homework
☐	☐	☐	☐	d. go to a club room

B. Scan the reading on pages 129–130 and complete the chart.

PREVIEWING CHART

Title of the article: _____

Names of people and places in the article
(List three more.)
Seoul, Korea _____
_____
_____
_____

Key words (What word appears several times? List three more.)
class _____
_____
_____
_____

I think the reading is about _____

---

[2] **How likely is it** How probable is it; How common is it

A DAY IN THE LIFE OF A FRESHMAN

by Chang Jae-Hyuk

*Chang Jae-Hyuk wrote this story when he was a university student in **Seoul, Korea**. Approximately 10.3 million people live in and around Seoul.*

Wednesday

1   **7:00 a.m.:** I get up about seven o'clock in the morning. Since my friends and I have a group blind date[3] with students from a women's university tonight, I take extra time to look my best. My mom calls me to eat breakfast, but I don't think I can. It's already 7:30 and I don't
5   want to be late for my 9:00 class. It takes me about an hour and a half to get to my university, so I hurry out.

8:00–9:00 a.m.: I take the bus to the subway station. There are so many people in the bus that I can't breathe. There is so much traffic that the bus can only crawl along.[4] Finally, the bus arrives at the
10   subway station. Unfortunately, there are a lot of people on the train and the air is stuffy. We finally arrive at Shinchon station and my university is now about a ten-minute walk away. I run to my philosophy class so I won't be late again. I have already missed this class four times.

9:00–11:00 a.m.: Thank goodness, I'm safe. The professor comes
15   in just after me.[5] But now I'm so tired from running that I can't concentrate. Then the person next to me asks what the homework is for our English class. That's right, there was English homework, but I forgot to do it! So I spend philosophy class doing my English homework.

English class is next. It seems like English is one big mountain that
20   we all have to get over in our university days. If we want to get a decent job, we have to be really good in English.

11:00 a.m.–2:00 p.m.: After two classes it's now 11:00, and I decide to go to my club room. Our **club members** spend their free time hanging out in that room. I chit chat[6] with my friends for a while and
25   then go to one of our school cafeterias for lunch.

---

[3] **a group blind date**   a date the writer and his friends have with a group of girls they don't know

[4] **crawl along**   move forward slowly

[5] **just after me**   a very short time after me

[6] **chit chat**   talk casually about unimportant things

2:00–5:30 p.m.: Now it's 2:00 and I have one more class at 3:00. My friends and I decide not to go to our 3:00 class. I shouldn't do this, but we don't want to hurry to the women's university after class. Instead, we go to play some **billiards** until it's time to go.

30 **5:30–10:30 p.m.:** It's 5:30 in a **coffee shop** in front of the university. All four of us are excited and wondering[7] what the girls will be like. About ten minutes later, four girls come in. Then the awkward time begins. We ask some questions and so do they. I find my dream girl sitting in the corner, but I don't have the guts[8] to speak to her.

35 After twenty minutes, it's time to choose our partners. We decide, at the count of three,[9] to point at the partner we would like to have. If a boy and a girl are pointing at each other, they become partners. One, two, three! My dream girl is also pointing at me!

I spend the evening with my partner having a wonderful time. Right

40 before we part, I ask for her phone number. If she gives me her number, that means she also likes me. And she does! I get home about 10:30. I'm very tired but really happy, hoping that things go well with her.

After You Read

Understanding the Text

A. What's the reason? What reason does the author give for each of the statements below? Circle the best answer.

1. In the story, the author doesn't eat breakfast because _____.

    a. he's not hungry

    b. he's late for class

    c. he doesn't want to be late for class

2. He says it's hard to breathe on the bus because _____.

    a. there are a lot of people on the bus

    b. the bus moves very slowly

    c. he had to run to the bus station

3. He can't concentrate in his philosophy class because _____.

    a. he missed four classes

    b. he is very tired

    c. he got to class safely

---

[7] **wondering** thinking about
[8] **the guts** the courage
[9] **at the count of three** after saying 1, 2, 3

4. He doesn't go to his 3 o'clock class because _____.

   a. he wants to have lunch in the cafeteria

   b. he doesn't want to hurry to his group date

   c. he didn't do his homework

5. It's uncomfortable at the beginning of the group date because _____.

   a. the girls are late

   b. the boys and girls don't know each other

   c. the boys and girls are good friends

B. Making inferences. Read the statements and check (√) True or False.

	True	False
1. You can infer that the author doesn't enjoy his daily trip to school.	☐	☐
2. You can infer that the author listened closely to his philosophy teacher.	☐	☐
3. You can infer that the author thinks it is important to study English.	☐	☐
4. You can infer that the author is a serious student.	☐	☐

C. Consider the issues. Work with a partner to answer the questions below.

1. How would you describe the university freshman on pages 129–130? Make five sentences with words from columns A and B.

   Example: *I think he is shy because he doesn't have the guts to speak to the girls.*

	A		B
	shy		skips classes.
	friendly		is often late to class.
	cool		doesn't listen in class.
I think	foolish	because	does his homework in class.
he is	disorganized	he	spends time with his friends.
	funny		knows how to play billiards.
			doesn't have the guts to speak to the girls.
	_____		_____
	_____		_____
	_____		

2. The author of the article on pages 129–130 says, "If we want to get a decent job, we have to be really good in English." What reasons might he give for this? Add two reasons to the list below.

English is necessary for getting a job because _____.

- *you might have to send an e-mail message in English*
- _____
- _____

Reading Skill

Using context clues

You can often guess the general meaning of a difficult word by looking at the context—the other words in the sentence or nearby sentences. In the examples below, the <u>underlined</u> words help you guess the meaning of the **boldfaced** words.

Examples:
The bus can only **crawl** along <u>because there is a lot of traffic.</u>
The air is **stuffy** <u>because the windows are closed.</u>
I can't **concentrate** on what the professor is saying <u>because I'm so tired from running to class.</u>

A. Use context to guess the missing words. Circle the correct letter.

1. Several people _____ because it was so cold yesterday.

    a. didn't wear coats

    b. felt good

    c. got sick

2. I feel like I _____ because there are so many people in the room and the windows are closed.

    a. can't breathe

    b. can't hear

    c. can't see

3. I ran to my class because I didn't want to be _____ again.

    a. early

    b. late

    c. on time

4. The ground was _____ because it rained all night.

  a. wet

  b. dry

  c. flat

5. I couldn't _____ his face because it was so dark.

  a. feel

  b. hear

  c. see

B. Use context to guess **the general meaning** of the boldfaced words.

  1. Several people **fainted** because it was so hot in the room.

  a. lost consciousness

  b. were happy

  c. had fun

  2. I feel like I **am suffocating** because there are so many people in the room.

  a. am able to breathe

  b. am not able to breathe

  c. am able to relax

  3. I ran to my class because I didn't want to be **tardy** again.

  a. early

  b. late

  c. on time

  4. The ground was **soggy** because it rained all night.

  a. dry

  b. hot

  c. wet

  5. I couldn't **make out** his face because it was so dark.

  a. hear

  b. feel

  c. see

Understanding two-word verbs

Some verbs have two words. For example, *put off*, *look after*, and *look up* are called two-word verbs.

The meaning of a two-word verb is different from the meaning of each word separately.

Examples:

- Our club members spend their free time **hanging out** in that room. (*hanging out = relaxing*)

- You should say goodbye before **hanging up** the telephone. (*hanging up = putting the telephone down*)

- **Hang on** for a minute while I look for my glasses. (*hang on = wait*)

- I can't **hang out** the clothes because it's raining. (*hang out = put wet clothes outdoors to dry*)

A. Read the sentences below and use context to guess the meaning of the boldfaced two-word verbs.

1. I hear your brother is **starting up** a new business. Are you going to work for him?

    a. creating

    b. losing

    c. selling

2. My English teacher usually **starts off** class by telling a funny story.

    a. misses

    b. begins

    c. creates

3. She walked outside, **started up** her motorcycle, and left.

    a. turned on

    b. turned off

    c. turned up

B. Choose six words from the reading that you want to remember. Add them to your vocabulary log on page 175.

Expressing cause and effect with <u>so</u> + noun/adjective + <u>that</u>

A cause and effect statement tells why something happens. We often use "*so* + noun/adjective + *that*" in a cause and effect statement. In the examples below, the cause is **boldfaced** and the effect is <u>underlined</u>.

- **There are so many people on the bus** that <u>I can't breathe</u>.
  (*I can't breathe because there are so many people on the bus.*)

- **There is so much traffic** that <u>the bus can only crawl along</u>.
  (*The bus can only crawl along because there is so much traffic.*)

- **I'm so tired** that <u>I can't concentrate</u>.
  (*I can't concentrate because I am very tired.*)

A. Rewrite these sentences with **so** + noun/adjective + **that**.

> **Example:**   I had to put my coat on because it was so cold inside.
>
> *It was so cold inside that I had to put my coat on.*

1. It's hard to work because it's so hot.

_____

2. I can't sleep because I drank so much coffee.

_____

3. I can't take a vacation because I have so much work to do.

_____

4. He fell asleep in class because he was so tired.

_____

5. I was late to class because there was so much traffic.

_____

B. Complete these sentences with a possible effect.

1. I'm so tired that I _____

2. I ate so much yesterday that I _____

3. He has so much money that he _____

4. It's so hot today that _____

Discussion & Writing

A. What do you do with friends after work or school? Check (√) **often, sometimes, rarely,** or **never.** Add one idea of your own to the list.

OFTEN	SOMETIMES	RARELY	NEVER	
☐	☐	☐	☐	hang out at school with friends
☐	☐	☐	☐	hang out at a friend's house
☐	☐	☐	☐	hang out in a coffee shop
☐	☐	☐	☐	play billiards
☐	☐	☐	☐	go shopping with friends
☐	☐	☐	☐	go to the movies with friends
☐	☐	☐	☐	study with friends
☐	☐	☐	☐	go on a group blind date
☐	☐	☐	☐	_____

B. What are the three best ways to find a boyfriend or girlfriend? Check (√) your answers. Add one idea of your own to the list.

☐ go on a blind date (you and your date only)

☐ go on a group blind date

☐ answer a personal ad

☐ place a personal ad

☐ join a club or group

☐ ask a friend to introduce you to someone

☐ talk in an Internet chat room

☐ hang out at a coffee shop

☐ _____

Compare your answers with a partner.

C. Write about a typical day in your life. Answer these questions in your writing:

- When do you get up on a typical day?
- How do you get to school or work?
- Is your trip relaxing or stressful?
- What are three interesting things you do during the day?
- When, where, and what do you eat on a typical day?

Example:

On a typical day, I get up at 7:30 a.m. I take a shower, get dressed, and have breakfast. Then, I walk to the subway and . . .

WORDS TO REMEMBER		
NOUNS	**VERBS**	**ADJECTIVES**
cafeteria	breathe	shy
(go on a)date	go (well)	foolish
partner	hang out	dull
subway station	hurry	stressful
traffic	look my best	tardy
(a ten-minute) walk	miss (a class)	
	point at	
	take time	

Chapter 14 Great Places to Visit

A beach on Lan Yu (Orchid Island), Taiwan, R.O.C.

There's no place like home.

—*English expression*

Chapter Focus

CONTENT:
Travel destinations

READING SKILL:
Reading words in chunks

BUILDING VOCABULARY:
Using context to know if a word is a noun or verb

LANGUAGE FOCUS:
Understanding *-ing* clauses

Before You Read

A. Choose one photograph on page 138, 140 or 141. Tell a partner three things you see.

> **Example:**
>
> *In the picture on page 140, I see a lot of people,*
> *a lot of food, and some tables with bowls of noodles.*

B. Scan the reading on pages 139–141 and complete the chart.

PREVIEWING CHART

Title of the article: _____

Names of people and places in the article (List three more.)	**Key words** (What words appear several times? List three more.)
Taiwan	market
_____	_____
_____	_____
_____	_____

I think the reading is about _____
_____

Reading Passage

GREAT PLACES TO VISIT

1   *Each month, **National Geographic Magazine** asks an editor from one of its international editions to answer the question, "What are the best places to visit in your area of the world?"*
5   *Yung Shih Lee, the editor of **National Geographic Taiwan,** thinks the sights below are some of the best places to visit in Taiwan. Would you like to visit these places?*

Shih-lin Night Market

"This market is the center of Taiwanese nightlife on the north side of **Taipei.** It's very
10 different from the morning markets where people shop for food to cook at home. At the Shih-lin Night Market, people show up[1] to have
15 a snack or drink, buy a few things, and just hang around.[2] Life really begins around 6 p.m. and can go on until three in the morning. On weekends the market is open even later."

Taroko Gorge[3]

"The word *taroko* means "beautiful"
20 in the language of the **Atayal** people and that's exactly what the Taroko Gorge is. Visitors can take a train or a 30-minute flight from Taipei to visit this natural wonder.[4] A 12-mile (19-
25 kilometer) bus tour takes passengers through the gorge, making stops for riders to walk through man-made tunnels[5] or enjoy the scenic views."

Lan Yu (Orchid Island)

"This small island about
30 40 miles (60 kilometers) southeast of Taiwan is home to the native **Yami** people. It is one of the few places in Taiwan
35 where the traditions of native people are still well preserved. Tourists can stay in island hotels or

Yami women dancing on Lan Yu

---

[1] **show up**   arrive at a place

[2] **hang around**   stay in one place without doing anything

[3] **gorge**   a deep, narrow opening between two mountains

[4] **natural wonder**   something in nature that you admire

[5] **tunnels**   holes through mountains for cars or trains

arrange to stay in a Yami family's home. Lan Yu is also home to many
40 species[6] found nowhere else in the world. Its beautiful coral reefs[7]
are also great for scuba diving."

The National Palace Museum

"When the **Chinese Nationalists** lost the civil war[8] in the late
1940s, they went to Taiwan, taking the imperial treasures[9] with them.
These treasures are now housed at the National Palace Museum in
45 Taipei. It's the best collection of Chinese artifacts[10] in the world. So if
visitors want to know more about the cultural heritage[11] of China,
this is the place to go. However, it takes a few days to see the museum
at a leisurely pace."[12]

---

[6] **species**   types of plants and animals

[7] **coral reefs**   lines of colorful rocks found in the sea

[8] **civil war**   a war between two groups in one country

[9] **imperial treasures**   valuable things that belonged to the empire

[10] **artifacts**   things that are interesting because of their history

[11] **cultural heritage**   traditions and achievements

[12] **at a leisurely pace**   without hurrying

After You Read

Understanding the Text

A. Multiple choice. For each item below, circle the best answer.

1. This reading is primarily about _____.

   a. beautiful places to visit in one city

   b. good places to visit in Taiwan

   c. good places to visit around the world

2. The author's purpose in writing this article was to _____.

   a. give useful information about interesting places in Taiwan

   b. tell an interesting story

   c. help people understand the history of Taiwan

3. You can infer that the National Palace Museum is _____.

   a. small

   b. large

   c. new

4. You can infer that Lan Yu (Orchid Island) _____.

   a. has a lot of natural beauty

   b. is a crowded place

   c. is a modern place

5. In line 5 of the reading passage, the word *sights* means _____.

   a. ability to see

   b. views

   c. places

6. In line 17, the words *go on* mean _____.

   a. continue

   b. leave

   c. get on

7. In line 33, the pronoun *it* refers to _____.

    a. Yami people

    b. Taiwan

    c. Lan Yu (Orchid Island)

B. Consider the issues. Work with a partner to answer the questions below.

    1. Use the information in the reading and pictures on pages 140–141 to complete the chart below. Then compare charts with a classmate.

PLACES TO VISIT IN TAIWAN	WHAT CAN YOU DO AND SEE THERE?
Shih-lin Night Market	• You can have a snack or drink.
	• You can see a lot of people.
	• _____
	• _____
The National Palace Museum	• You can see lots of Chinese artifacts.
	• _____
	• _____
	• _____
Lan Yu (Orchid Island)	• _____
	• _____
	• _____
	• _____
Taroko Gorge	• _____
	• _____
	• _____
	• _____

    2. Use your notes from the activity above to answer these questions.

        a. Which of these places would be interesting to a young child? Why?

        b. Which place would help foreigners understand life in Taiwan today? Why?

        c. Which place would be the most interesting to you? Why?

> **Reading words in chunks**
> We don't usually read a sentence word by word. Instead, we read words in "chunks," or groups. Reading words in chunks makes it easier to understand the ideas in a sentence.
>
> **Example:**
>
> - Reading word by word: *It's / very / different / from / the / . . .*
>
> - Reading in chunks: *It's very different from / the morning markets / where people shop for food / to cook at home.*
>
> Here are some common chunks of words:
>
> - article + adjective + noun:
>   *the morning markets; the cultural heritage; the imperial treasures*
> - dependent clauses:
>   *where people shop for food; that everybody likes*
> - infinitive + noun:
>   *to cook food; to make a mistake*
> - prepositional phrases:
>   *at a leisurely pace; in a restaurant*
> - verb + adverb:
>   *are now housed; left quietly*

A. Read aloud each pair of sentences one chunk at a time. Check (√) the sentence that sounds more natural to you.

☐ 1a. When the / Chinese Nationalists moved to / Taiwan, they / took the imperial / treasures with them.

☑ 1b. When the Chinese Nationalists / moved to Taiwan, / they took the imperial treasures / with them.

☐ 2a. Visitors can take a train / or a 30-minute flight / from Taipei / to visit this natural wonder.

☐ 2b. Visitors can / take a train or a 30-minute / flight from Taipei to / visit this natural wonder.

□ 3a. Life really begins / around six p.m. / and can go on / until three in the morning.

□ 3b. Life really begins around six / p.m. and can go on until / three in the morning.

B. Read aloud the paragraphs below. Where do you pause or take a breath? Mark each chunk of words with a slash (/). Use the first paragraph as an example. More than one answer is possible.

Each month,/**National Geographic Magazine** asks an editor/ from one of its international editions/to answer the question,/ *What are the best places to visit/in your area of the world?*/ Yungshih Lee, /the editor of **National Geographic Taiwan**,/thinks the sights below/are some of the best places to visit/in Taiwan. Would you like/to visit these places?

Shih-lin Night Market
"This market is the center of Taiwanese nightlife on the north side of **Taipei**. It's very different from the morning markets where people shop for food to cook at home. At the Shih-lin Night Market, people show up to have a snack or drink, buy a few things, and just hang around. Life really begins around six p.m. and can go on until three in the morning. On weekends the market is open even later."

The National Palace Museum
"When the **Chinese Nationalists** lost the civil war in the late 1940s, they went to Taiwan, taking the imperial treasures with them. These treasures are now housed at the National Palace Museum in Taipei. It's the best collection of Chinese artifacts in the world. So if visitors want to know more about the cultural heritage of China, this is the place to go. However, it takes a few days to see the museum at a leisurely pace.

Compare your ideas with a partner.

Using context to know if a word is a noun or verb
Many nouns and verbs in English have the same form.
For example, the word *house* can be both a noun and a verb. You must use context to know if the word is a noun or verb.

Example:

• They decided to **house** the imperial treasures at the National Palace Museum. *("House" is a verb.)*

• Would you prefer to live in a **house** or an apartment? *("House" is a noun.)*

Here are some other words that you can use as a noun or a verb:

cook	shop	treasure
e-mail	sleep	visit
place	steam	walk
request		

A. In each question, is the word in italics a noun or a verb? Circle **noun** or **verb**.

1. Which of your possessions do you *treasure* the most? (noun / verb)

2. What shouldn't you *place* on your desk during a test? (noun / verb)

3. Where would you *house* ten students visiting from another country? (noun / verb)

4. Did you make any *stops* on your way to class today? (noun / verb)

5. How often do you go for a *walk*? (noun / verb)

6. Do you think it's important to get enough *sleep*? (noun / verb)

7. Do you know how to *steam* fish? (noun / verb)

8. Where do you *shop* for clothes? (noun / verb)

9. What do you know how to *cook*? (noun / verb)

10. Would you rather live in a *house* or an apartment? (noun / verb)

B. Pair work. Ask a partner the questions in Activity A.

C. Choose six words from the reading that you want to remember. Add them to your vocabulary log on page 175.

Understanding **-ing** clauses

Writers use *-ing* clauses to help readers form a mental picture of something. These clauses are common in descriptive writing. They are not common in spoken English. In each sentence below, the boldfaced words form an *-ing* clause.

Examples:

- A bus tour takes passengers through the gorge, **making stops for riders to walk through the tunnels.**

- When the Chinese Nationalists lost the civil war, they went to Taiwan, **taking the imperial treasures with them.**

A. Choose the **-ing** clause that best completes each sentence. Write the number of the sentence.

Sentences	-ing clause
1. The plane crashed,	__ looking at each other.
2. The nuclear reactor exploded,	__ taking her daughter with her.
3. The girls and boys sat around the table,	_1_ killing the pilot and flight engineer.
4. He came to the meeting,	__ yelling "Charge!"
5. She went to the concert hall,	__ wearing his best suit.
6. The fans cheered,	__ leaking radiation into the atmosphere.

B. Rewrite each sentence, using an **-ing** clause.

1. We stood inside the room we built, and we felt a sense of fulfillment.

> **Example:** *We stood inside the room we built, feeling a sense of fulfillment.*

2. He stayed up all night, and watched TV.

3. She answered her mobile phone, and held her hand over her mouth.

A. Think of an example for each type of place below. Your places can be anywhere in the world.

TYPE OF PLACE	WHERE (CITY OR COUNTRY)
1. a natural wonder	
Example:	
the Grand Canyon	the United States
2. a man-made wonder	
3. a museum	
4. a market	

Share ideas with your classmates.

Example:

The Grand Canyon in the United States is an example of a natural wonder.

B. Choose a town or city in your country. Identify three good places to visit there.

TOWN OR CITY: _____

PLACES	THINGS TO DO AND SEE THERE	
Example: San Francisco	• ride a bike	• picnic
Golden Gate Park	• rollerskate	• rent a boat
1.	•	•
	•	
2.	•	•
	•	
3.	•	•
	•	

C. Write a short description about the places you chose.

Example:

Great Places to Visit in ___San Francisco___

There are many great places to visit in San Francisco. One of my favorite places is Golden Gate Park. You can ride a bike, . . .

WORDS TO REMEMBER			
NOUNS	**VERBS**	**ADJECTIVES**	**ADVERBS**
collection	go on	natural	leisurely
heritage	have (a snack)	man-made	
island	lose (a war)	cultural	
market	make (a stop)		
museum	show up		
(at a leisurely) pace	hang around		
passengers			
sights			
species			
treasures			
view			
(a natural) wonder			

High school   *High school* students in the United States are generally 14–18 years old. All students in the United States must go to school until they are 16 years old. Here is a chart with more information about American high school students:

GRADE	NAME FOR STUDENTS	AGE OF STUDENTS
9	Freshman	14–15
10	Sophomore	15–16
11	Junior	16–17
12	Senior	17–18

Street sign   *Street signs* tell people the names of streets they are on. In the United States and many countries around the world, you find street signs on street corners in most cities and towns. Street signs help police officers and ambulance drivers find people's houses when there are emergencies.

Football   In most countries, *football* is a game in which two teams of players kick a round, white ball into a goal. Americans, however, call this game *soccer*, not football. In *American football*, two teams of players throw, run, and kick a brown ball back and forth. Famous American football teams include the Dallas Cowboys, the San Francisco 49ers, and the New York Giants.

Japan *Japan* is an island nation in northeast Asia. The capital of Japan is Tokyo. About 25 million people live in and around the city. The population of Japan is about 127 million. Japan has the second largest economy in the world after the United States. People from Japan are called *Japanese*, and the language they speak is also called Japanese.

London *London* is the capital of the United Kingdom, an island nation in the North Atlantic Ocean. The United Kingdom includes England, Scotland, Wales, and Northern Ireland. About seven million people live in London.

Potatoes In England, the United States, and other Western countries, many people eat *potatoes* with dinner every night. *French fries*, *baked potatoes*, and *mashed potatoes* are the most popular potato dishes in the United States. People eat potatoes with meat, chicken, and fish.

Pub In England and other countries, *pubs* are casual places to eat, drink, and talk to friends. A favorite pub meal is *fish and chips*. This is a meal of fried fish and potatoes that many people enjoy with beer. In the United States, pubs are not common. Many American adults meet their friends for drinks at a *bar*, and then go to a restaurant for dinner.

Internet   With the *Internet*, you can find information on any topic. The Internet has thousands of *Web sites* containing information about companies, organizations, and people. If you want information about Taiwanese food, for example, you type the words "Taiwanese food" into a *search engine* like *Yahoo!* The search engine shows you many Web sites with information on Taiwanese food. When you click on each of these Web sites, you can read and learn about Taiwanese food.

Massachusetts Institute of Technology   The *Massachusetts Institute of Technology* is often called "MIT." It is located in Cambridge, Massachusetts, near Boston. MIT is one of the best and most famous universities in the world for students interested in science, engineering, and technology. There are about 10,000 students at MIT.

India   *India* is located in southern Asia between Pakistan and Burma. India's coastline along the Arabian Sea and Bay of Bengal is 7000 kilometers long. More than one billion people live in India. The capital of India is New Delhi, which has a population of ten million people. Many Indian people speak English because India was once a British colony. Hindi, however, is the national language.

KFC   *KFC* is a popular fast food restaurant in North America, Asia, and other parts of the world. Many people think KFC serves delicious fried chicken. The original name of KFC was *Kentucky Fried Chicken*. Kentucky is a state in the eastern part of the United States.

English-speaking country   An *English-speaking country* is a country in which many or most people speak English. English is the *official language*, or one of the official languages, in an English-speaking country. Canada, England, Australia, and the United States are all English-speaking countries.

Canada   *Canada* is the very large country north of the United States in North America. Thirty-one million people live there. The capital of Canada is Ottawa, and the largest cities are Toronto, Montreal, and Vancouver. The official languages of Canada are English and French.

Volunteer work   When you do *volunteer work*, you help other people, but you don't get paid. Many people do volunteer work in schools, hospitals, and museums. For example, volunteers read books to sick people in hospitals or help teachers in a classroom.

Tourist center   At *tourist centers*, you can find maps and other information about places you are visiting. Most large cities around the world have tourist centers that provide tourist information in many languages.

Night club   A *night club* is a place where people go at night to meet friends, have drinks, and dance. Night clubs have a dance floor, while *bars* don't. Other names for night clubs are *clubs* or *discos*. You must be 21 years old to go to most night clubs in the United States. Twenty-one is the legal drinking age in the United States. In Canada, the legal drinking age is 18 years old in some parts of the country, and 19 in other parts.

Bartender   A *bartender* is the man or woman who stands behind the bar and serves drinks at a night club, restaurant, or bar.

Quarters   A *quarter* is a Canadian or American coin with a value of 25 cents. There are 100 cents in a dollar ($1.00). Here are the names and values of the four common Canadian and American coins:

NAME	VALUE
Penny	1 cent ($.01)
Nickel	5 cents ($.05)
Dime	10 cents ($.10)
Quarter	25 cents ($.25)

Health professionals   *Health professionals* are people who work in the medical field. *Doctors, nurses, dentists,* and *psychologists* are all health professionals.

Negative publicity   A company gets *negative publicity* when something bad happens to its products, services, or employees. For example, a restaurant can get negative publicity if someone gets sick after eating there.

Traveling salesman   A *traveling salesman* is a person who goes to many different towns and cities to sell his company's products or services. *Salesman* refers to a *man* who sells things, while *saleswoman* refers to a *woman* who works in sales. In the United States and other countries, the term *salesperson* is often used. A salesperson can be a man *or* a woman who sells things.

Radiation   *Radiation* happens when one object sends heat or energy to another object. *Heat radiation* from the sun, for example, is heat sent from the sun to the earth. A cell phone sends *microwave radiation* from the phone into the brain of the person talking on it. Many studies have shown that this radiation may be dangerous for the brain.

Warning label   A *warning label* is a small piece of paper on the outside of a product. This label tells people that the product may be dangerous. In many countries, there are warning labels on packages of cigarettes. The warning label on cigarettes sold in the United States says: "WARNING: Cigarette smoking is dangerous to your health."

Everglades The *Everglades National Park* is a large area in southern Florida, near Miami. Much of this area is covered by water. The Everglades looks like a forest because a lot of trees are growing there, but these trees are growing out of the water. People can take boat rides through the Everglades to see the beautiful trees, plants, and pink birds called *flamingos*.

First-class section Many planes have two sections — a *first-class section* and an *economy section*. First-class passengers enjoy better food and service than economy passengers. The first-class section also has larger seats and more space for your legs. Larger planes often have three sections: first-class, *business*, and economy. The business section is more expensive than economy, but cheaper than first-class.

Flight attendant *Flight attendants* are responsible for your safety on a plane. They also serve food and drinks. The term *flight attendant* is used for men and women. Here are some of the minimum qualifications to be a flight attendant with United Airlines, one of the largest American airlines. You must:

- have a neat, conservative, professional appearance
- be at least 19 years old
- have a high school diploma
- not be taller than 6'2" (1.83 meters)

Safety tests Cars, planes, and many other products must pass *safety tests* before they are sold. Safety tests help companies see if products are safe for people to use. Companies want to make sure people will not be injured by their products.

Volunteer A *volunteer* is someone who helps other people, but doesn't get paid. According to an American study called *Giving and Volunteering in the United States*, 56% of Americans did volunteer work in 1999. The Japan Broadcasting Corporation reports that 26% of Japanese people did volunteer work in 1998.

Philippines The *Philippines* is an island nation in southeast Asia. (Note: English speakers call this country *the* Philippines.) Manila is the capital city. The population of the Philippines is 83 million, and 83% of the people are Roman Catholic. People from the Philippines are called *Filipinos*. The country has two official languages: Filipino and English.

Nishinomiya, Japan *Nishinomiya City* is located in the southeastern part of Hyogo Prefecture in Japan between Kobe and Osaka. About 450,000 people live in Nishinomiya. This city is famous for producing *Pure Nada Sake. Sake* is a popular Japanese drink.

Negros Island, Philippines *Negros Island* is located in the southern part of the Philippines. About one million people live on the island. Negros Island is near Cebu, the famous island resort. Agriculture is the main activity of the people on Negros Island. They grow sugar, corn, coconut, and rice.

Foreign baseball players *Foreign baseball players* are players who are citizens of one country, but play baseball in another country. For example, an American playing baseball in Japan is a foreign baseball player.

Venezuela *Venezuela* is a large country in South America. It is located on the Caribbean Sea and North Atlantic Ocean next to Colombia. The capital of Venezuela is Caracas. Twenty-four million people live in Venezuela and the official language is Spanish. Baseball is very popular in Venezuela.

Taiwan *Taiwan, R.O.C.* (Republic of China) is an island state located off the coast of southeastern China. The population of Taiwan is about 23 million. Taipei is the capital of Taiwan and is located on the northern part of the island. People from Taiwan are called *Taiwanese*. Mandarin Chinese is the official language of Taiwan.

Hot dogs *Hot dogs* are warm red sausages that Americans eat at baseball, football, and other games. People usually eat hot dogs in a piece of white bread called a *roll*. Many people put *ketchup*, *mustard*, and *onions* on their hot dogs.

Popcorn *Popcorn* is a snack that many Americans enjoy at professional sports events, at the movies, and many other places. Popcorn is white and light. Some people put butter and salt on their popcorn.

Dominican Republic The *Dominican Republic* is located on an island in the Caribbean Sea. (Note: English speakers call this country *the* Dominican Republic.) Santo Domingo is the country's capital. About 8.5 million people live in the Dominican Republic. People from this country are called *Dominicans*, and Spanish is the official language.

Merengue *Merengue* is a very popular Dominican dance. The man and woman dance close together. They move their hips from left to right. Merengue music is very fast and happy. When you hear it, you want to dance.

Singapore *Singapore* is a small island nation next to Malaysia in Southeast Asia. About 4.5 million people live in Singapore. People from Singapore are called *Singaporeans*. Chinese and English are the official languages.

Thailand *Thailand* is a large country in southeast Asia. The country borders Burma, Cambodia, Laos, and Malaysia. About 62 million people live in Thailand. The capital of the country is Bangkok. People from Thailand are called *Thai*. Their language is also called Thai.

Central Conservatory of China *The Central Conservatory of China* is one of the most famous schools for studying music in China.

Royal College of Music Musicians from all over the world study at the *Royal College of Music* in London, England. Young musicians, aged 8–18, study in the Junior Department at the college.

Mozart Wolfgang Amadeus Mozart (1756–1791) is one of the most important composers of classical music. Mozart was born in Salzburg, Austria. He is called a *child prodigy* because he composed beautiful music and was a great piano player when he was only six years old.

Mendelssohn Felix Mendelssohn (1809–1847) was also a *child prodigy* and a great composer. Mendelssohn was born in Hamburg, Germany. Like Mozart, Mendelssohn was an excellent composer and piano player when he was a young boy.

Germany *Germany* is Europe's richest country. With 83 million people, Germany has the largest population of all of the European countries. Germany borders nine countries, including France and Poland. The capital of Germany is Berlin. People from Germany are called *Germans*, and their language is called German, too.

Music charts People look at *music charts* every week to see which songs are the most popular. These charts are often called *Top 20 charts* because they list the twenty most popular songs for the past week. You can find Top 20 charts in magazines, newspapers, and on Web sites. In the United States, the most popular Top 20 chart is published every week by *Billboard*. Billboard has Top 20 charts for many kinds of music including pop, country, electronic, and rap.

Chapter 11 – Culture and Language Notes

Three Mile Island   There is a famous nuclear plant at *Three Mile Island* in Pennsylvania. Pennsylvania is near New York on the east coast of the United States. Most Americans were afraid when they first heard about the nuclear accident at Three Mile Island in 1979. Since the accident, Americans have discussed the safety of nuclear power a lot. Nuclear power is still used in the United States. However, no nuclear power plants have been built in the United States since the Three Mile Island accident in 1979.

The Soviet Union   The Soviet Union was formed in 1917 after the Russian Revolution. It was a very large country between northern Europe and China. (Note: English speakers call this former country *the* Soviet Union.) Nowadays, the *former Soviet Union* includes many different countries, for example, Russia, Latvia, and Uzbekistan.

World War II   The largest war in the history of the world was *World War II*. World War II was fought between 1939 and 1945. In this war, England, the Soviet Union, the United States, and other countries defeated Germany, Italy, and Japan.

Chapter 12 – Culture and Language Notes

(None for this Chapter)

Seoul, Korea *Seoul* is the capital of the Republic of Korea. About 10.3 million people live in Seoul, one of the biggest cities in Asia. Seoul is the largest city in Korea, a country with a population of 47 million. People around the world learned a lot about Seoul when the 1988 Summer Olympic Games were played in that city.

Thank goodness Many English speakers use the expression *Thank goodness*. They use this expression to say they feel happy, lucky, or relieved. For example, if there is a car accident and no one is hurt, people say, "Thank goodness! No one was hurt."

Club members Students at schools and universities throughout the world join *clubs*. Clubs are groups of people who share the same interests. For example, students who like to study French can join a French club. The students in a club are called *club members*.

Billiards *Billiards* is a game played on a table with hard, round balls. (Note: The word *billiards* is always used with a singular verb: *Billiards* is fun.) There are several forms of billiards games including *pool* and *snookers*. In each of these games, you use a *cue* — or a long stick — to hit one ball against another ball. The goal is to send all of your balls into holes on the sides and corners of the table. Billiards was originally played in Europe more than 500 years ago, but it is now popular all over the world.

Coffee shop A *coffee shop* is a casual and inexpensive place to get coffee and a snack or a meal. Coffee shops are popular places at which students all over the world hang out. On many American university campuses, you can find *coffee shops*, snack bars, ice cream shops, and/or fast food restaurants like McDonald's or KFC.

National Geographic Magazine   *The National Geographic Society* is the world's largest non-profit organization for science and education. Every month, this society publishes a magazine with beautiful photographs and articles about people, animals, and interesting places from all over the world. *National Geographic* is published in many different languages, including Chinese, Korean, and Japanese.

Taipei   Taipei is the capital of Taiwan, Republic of China, an island off the coast of southeastern China. About six million people live in and around Taipei. From the city, you can see mountains to the north, in Yangmingshan National Park. Taipei is a busy and exciting city known for its friendly people and excellent food.

Atayal   The *Atayal* people live in northern Taiwan. They are one of the nine tribes or groups of people who have lived on the island of Taiwan for hundreds of years. Many Atayal people live inside the Taroko National Park, about 40 miles (64 kilometers) from Taipei. The men are good hunters and the women are excellent weavers.

Yami   The *Yami* people have lived on Lan Yu (Orchid Island) for thousands of years. The people still live very traditionally with no cars, banks, or other signs of modern life. The Yami men wear silver helmets on their heads. The men with the largest helmets are the richest men in the group. The Yami people also build beautiful wooden boats. It often takes three years to build these boats because they have so much beautiful design and decoration.

Chinese Nationalists   In the late 1940s, there was a civil war in China between two groups: the Communists and the *Nationalists*. Chiang Kai-Shek (1887–1975) was the leader of the Nationalists. When Chiang and the Nationalists lost the war in China, they were forced to leave. They went to Taiwan, where Chiang became the leader. He led Taiwan from 1949 until his death in 1975.

Map 1 **Europe & the Former Soviet Union**

0   250   500 miles

0   250   500 kilometers

ATLANTIC
OCEAN

North
Sea

Baltic Sea

FORMER
SOVIET UNION

ENGLAND

GERMANY

London

Chernobyl

UKRAINE

SWITZERLAND

AUSTRIA

Black Sea

Mediterranean Sea

Map 2 **East Asia**

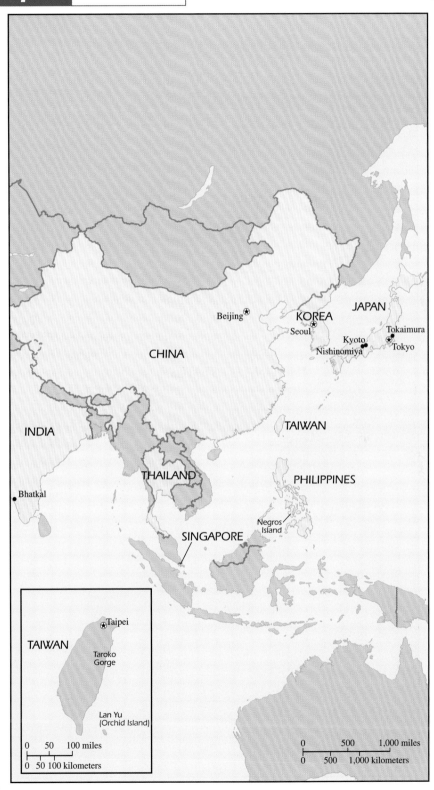

Beijing ✪

KOREA

JAPAN

Seoul ✪

CHINA

Kyoto ●

Tokaimura ✪

Nishinomiya

Tokyo

INDIA

TAIWAN

THAILAND

PHILIPPINES

Bhatkal ●

SINGAPORE

Negros
Island

✪Taipei

TAIWAN

Taroko
Gorge

Lan Yu
(Orchid Island)

0   50   100 miles

0   50 100 kilometers

0   500   1,000 miles

0   500   1,000 kilometers

Map 3 **North America**

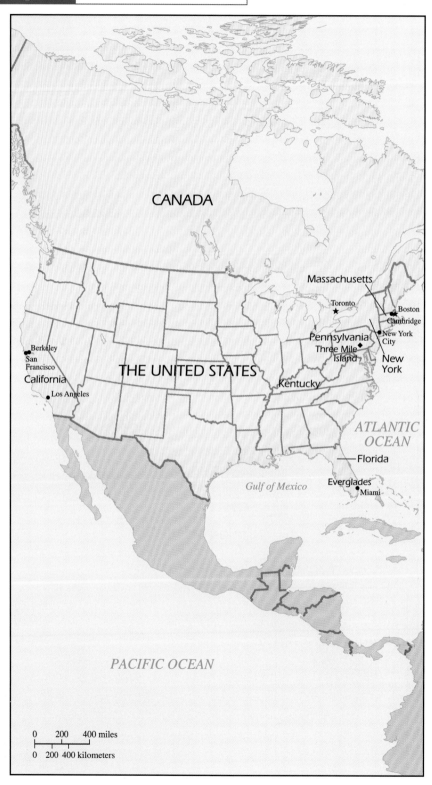

CANADA

THE UNITED STATES

Massachusetts

Toronto

Boston
Cambridge

Berkeley
San
Francisco

Pennsylvania
Three Mile
Island

New York
City

New
York

California

Los Angeles

Kentucky

ATLANTIC
OCEAN

Florida

Gulf of Mexico

Everglades
Miami

PACIFIC OCEAN

0   200   400 miles

0   200 400 kilometers

Map 4   South America

DOMINICAN
REPUBLIC

Caribbean Sea

ATLANTIC OCEAN

VENEZUELA

ATLANTIC OCEAN

PACIFIC
OCEAN

0	400	800 miles
0	400	800 kilometers

Present	Past	Past Participle
(be) am/is/are	was, were	been
bring	brought	brought
buy	bought	bought
come	came	come
cut	cut	cut
do	did	done
drink	drank	drunk
drive	drove	driven
eat	ate	eaten
fly	flew	flown
fall	fell	fallen
feel	felt	felt
get	got	gotten
give	gave	given
go	went	gone
grow	grew	grown
have	had	had
hear	heard	heard
keep	kept	kept
lose	lost	lost
make	made	made
meet	met	met
put	put	put
quit	quit	quit
read	read	read
ride	rode	ridden
run	ran	run
see	saw	seen
sell	sold	sold
set	set	set
sit	sat	sat
sleep	slept	slept
speak	spoke	spoken
spend	spent	spent
take	took	taken
teach	taught	taught
tell	told	told
think	thought	thought
wear	wore	worn
write	wrote	written

Chapter 1

Vocabulary Log

New word in context	My example
Example: *Some scientists think that sleep helps the body to <u>relieve stress.</u>*	*I think taking a walk helps relieve stress.*
1	
2	
3	
4	
5	
6	

Vocabulary Log

New word in context	My example
Example: *Their warm welcome made me feel <u>at ease.</u>*	*I don't feel at ease when I'm taking a test.*
1	
2	
3	
4	
5	
6	

Chapter 3 — Vocabulary Log

New word in context	My example
Example: *It seemed <u>likely</u> that computers would replace books.*	*It seems likely that we'll finish this book.*
1	
2	
3	
4	
5	
6	

Chapter 4 — Vocabulary Log

New word in context	My example
Example: *to <u>save money</u> on food*	*I need to save money for my trip.*
1	
2	
3	
4	
5	
6	

Chapter 5

Vocabulary Log

New word in context	My example
Example: *I <u>practiced</u> speaking English.*	*I need to practice giving speeches.*
1	
2	
3	
4	
5	
6	

Chapter 6 — Vocabulary Log

New word in context	My example
Example: *Phone companies <u>are worried about</u> the negative publicity.*	*I sometimes worry about making a mistake.*
1	
2	
3	
4	
5	
6	

Chapter **7** — **Vocabulary Log**

New word in context	My example
Example: *The man <u>ignored</u> the flight attendant.*	*I don't like it when people ignore me.*
1	
2	
3	
4	
5	
6	

Chapter **8** — **Vocabulary Log**

New word in context	My example
Example: *The people helped us <u>appreciate</u> the more valuable things in life.*	*I appreciate what I have.*
1	
2	
3	
4	
5	
6	

Chapter 9 — Vocabulary Log

New word in context	My example
Example: *The behavior of baseball fans is very different from country to country.*	*My teacher has never criticized my behavior in class.*
1	
2	
3	
4	
5	
6	

Chapter 10 — Vocabulary Log

New word in context	My example
Example: *She had to concentrate on just one instrument.*	*I need to concentrate on getting a job.*
1	
2	
3	
4	
5	
6	

Vocabulary Log

New word in context	My example
Example: *Three employees <u>accidentally</u> poured too much uranium into a tank.*	*I accidentally dropped my telephone.*
1	
2	
3	
4	
5	
6	

Vocabulary Log

New word in context	My example
Example: *We <u>made eye contact</u> and my heart began to beat faster.*	*I don't like to make eye contact with strangers.*
1	
2	
3	
4	
5	
6	

Vocabulary Log

New word in context	My example
Example: *My university is now about a ten-minute <u>walk</u> away.*	*My school is a five-minute walk from the subway.*
1	
2	
3	
4	
5	
6	

Vocabulary Log

New word in context	My example
Example: *At the Shih-lin Night Market, people show up to <u>have a snack</u> or a drink.*	*I like to have a snack before I go to bed.*
1	
2	
3	
4	
5	
6	

Vocabulary Index

Chapter 1

blurry
dangerous
effects (of)
experiment
find out
go without
have (trouble)
imagine
normal
pass (a test)
reasonable
recover (from)
spend (time)
stress

Chapter 2

advice
alone
delicious
do (research)
get used to
have (a party)
impressions
middle-class
realize
reasonable
reply
select
worry about
treat (someone) like

Chapter 3

a number of
appear
cheaper
comfortable
computers
convenient
electronic
entirely
experts
instantly

(the) Internet
inventions
likely
permanent
press
preview
replace
similar (to)
technology

Chapter 4

businessperson
company
dream
earn
end up
fail to
(work) hard
hope
impress
impressive
improve
job
lose (money)
manager
own
profit
profitable
save (money)
start out
succeed
success
successful
successfully
wonder

Chapter 5

communicate
disappointed
embarrassed
experience
have (trouble)
pronounce